THE TRUE LAW OF POPULATION

THE

TRUE LAW OF POPULATION

SHEWN AS CONNECTED WITH

THE FOOD OF THE PEOPLE

BY

THOMAS DOUBLEDAY

[1847]

REPRINTS OF ECONOMIC CLASSICS

AUGUSTUS M. KELLEY · PUBLISHERS
NEW YORK · 1967

First Edition 1841
Second Edition 1847
(London: George Peirce, *310 Strand*, 1847)

Reprinted 1967 by
AUGUSTUS M. KELLEY PUBLISHERS

Library of Congress Catalogue Card Number
67 - 17492

PRINTED IN THE UNITED STATES OF AMERICA
by SENTRY PRESS, NEW YORK, N. Y. 10019

THE

TRUE LAW OF POPULATION

SHEWN TO BE CONNECTED WITH THE

FOOD OF THE PEOPLE.

By THOMAS DOUBLEDAY, Esq.,

AUTHOR OF THE ITALIAN WIFE—BABINGTON—DIOCLESIAN—CAIUS MARIUS—
NORTHERN LIGHTS, ETC., ETC.

" *Old* Families last not THREE OAKS."
SIR THOMAS BROWNE.

SECOND EDITION.

LONDON:
GEORGE PEIRCE, 310, STRAND.

1847.

PREFACE.

OF the following work, the author may justly affirm, that perhaps no treatise, embodying a theory of a novel, and, at first sight, somewhat singular nature, was ever begun with fewer prejudices or preconceived notions relative to it, on the part of the writer. It was, indeed, purely by accident that the author was brought upon the train of thought, which, being pursued in all its ramifications, resulted in the present work. He by no means intends, of course, to assert that he had not at one time or other examined the various theories that have been put forth on the puzzling subject of Population, nor to deny that

he may have been bewildered by some, and
staggered by others. Still, for many years, this
subject, and the various views of it by various
writers, had been put aside as it were by him, as
matters with regard to which he was neither
prepared to record an assent or dissent : nor was
his scepticism lessened by the following admo-
nition. Happening, many years ago, in the
presence of a late relative, long since deceased,
remarkable both for the sagacity and extended
benevolence of his general views on philosophical
subjects, to draw some of those startling, though
not illogical, conclusions which seemed to flow
from theories then recently broached as to this
subject, and much in vogue at the time, the
reply was this :—" Depend upon it, my dear
nephew, that you and I may safely decline to
yield an implicit assent, though we may not on
the instant be able to refute them, to views from
which consequences such as you have drawn
legitimately flow. Though I may not live to see it,
nor you, a time will yet come when this mystery

will be unveiled ; and when a, perhaps now mysterious, but, beyond doubt, a beneficent law will
be discovered, regulating this matter, in accordance with all the rest that we see of God's moral
government of the world." This judgment, de-
livered with a solemnity and earnestness rather
unusual with the speaker, made a deep impression, and from that time forward, and for
many years after, the author regarded the question
of population as one of those insoluble problems
which are put in his way to humble the intellec-
tual pride of man, but at the same time to
stimulate his inquiry into the laws of his own
nature and of the creation around him, with a
humble reliance that, as heretofore, everything
which shall be unfolded will only show forth,
more and more, the wisdom and benevolence of
the great Architect of all things.

Chance, the author of these sheets has already
said, led him to stumble upon the chain of
reasoning, which, with its results, he now ven-

tures to lay before the Public. It may, on that account, probably be more easy to be believed by his readers, that, entering upon his researches without any preconcerted opinions or views as to the shape which they were to take, or the goal at which they were to arrive, he followed the clue of evidence with the sole wish of arriving, if possible, at the truth, unembarrassed by any accompanying considerations as to the bearings of that truth when discovered; being well convinced, where they are the bearings of truth, they must be good. In the course of this inquiry, however, be it begun under what circumstances it might, it has certainly been impossible for an inquirer not to perceive, from time to time, that the positions necessarily arrived at, sometimes as necessarily involved considerations connected with the general policy of nations, and the acts of Governments. This could not be avoided, because this is involved in the nature of the subject itself. When, however, the author has deemed it proper to draw collateral conclusions, as requisite to the full and complete elucidation of his subject, he has adhered to the rule of only deducing such general con- clusions as were plainly requisite for that purpose. Even of such conclusions he has drawn as few as possible, partly from the conviction that to load a general argument with minute collateral inference is ill-judged in the reasoner who does so ; and partly from a wish to keep his essay clear of those party conclusions, or political feelings, which, often as they have assisted to mar philosophical discussion, have never yet advanced it one single step.

Although, however, he disclaims any regard foreign to that for the truth, which ought to ac- tuate all writers, as mingling itself with his pursuit of the truth as to this question, the author yet is not disposed to deny that he felt both strengthened and encouraged in this course by the discovery that, as he proceeded step by step, the facts, as they unfolded themselves,

accorded with his general convictions of the
benevolence of the Deity, and the wonderful
providence by which, under the agency of an
unseen law, unrecognised, and unthought of, the
happiness of mankind is often regulated and
achieved upon a scale of moral government
of which the human eye can only see portions,
and which the human intellect can only compre-
hend in part. It has, indeed, ever been his creed
that the philosophy which is in admitted accordance with that benevolence which is the first
attribute of that great Being whose ways, however, are of necessity often inscrutable by His
creatures, has at all events the weight of *à priori*
recommendation in its favour—for although
that which may, to imperfect observers, seem
to militate against God's providence may be
true, that which accords with it must, as
far as such accordance is concerned ; and it
must ever be the case with paradoxes which
seem exceptions to the laws of Providence, that
they involve in themselves a contradiction

which, on the first showing, destroys their own existence; because, upon the postulate of the goodness of God, all reasoning, moral or physical, is ultimately and proximately founded, nor can such exist in connection with its denial.

The concluding Chapter of this volume will be found to treat of a class of subjects as to which the writer is avowedly unlearned. The considerations there detailed were rather forced upon than sought by him; and being so, he did not deem there was either impropriety or arrogance in describing views which may very possibly turn out to be erroneous and fanciful, provided they were uncontradicted by the writings of those versed in such knowledge, and qualified to speak with authority on questions of physiology. As far as the author can ascertain, he has not, in entertaining the peculiar notions there detailed, run counter to any fact laid down and admitted by physiologists or nosologists; and, therefore, neither coming, nor desirous to come in collision with any one, he may be readily pardoned for having, perhaps rashly, taken up views which, if they are unfounded, are at all events innocuous, inasmuch as, if not scientific in themselves, they do not seem to interfere with the science of others. If they do not help the author's argument, he trusts they may not hurt it, being in themselves perfectly extrinsic; and if true, only calculated to account for facts which have been already demonstrated.

Having commenced this work in a spirit of calm and candid inquiry, the author has judged it proper, if not necessary, to keep his style somewhat in accordance with his subject matter, and to write plainly, upon a dry, though important question. He is an inquirer, and not a partisan; and therefore, happily, as he deems it, excused from attempting either to recommend his theme by eloquence or the artifices of rhetoric, or to adorn it by the extraneous ornaments of figurative or florid composition. He trusts the judicious reader will not permit this to operate to his disadvantage, but the contrary; and, whilst treating a subject like this now under discussion, he cannot but think that he who would judge of his book from the ornaments of style it might or may not contain, is adopting a criterion little less strange, on such an occasion, than that of Heliogabalus, who is said to have formed his opinion of the City of Rome from the great quantity of cobwebs that were found in it.

In fine, this book is not addressed to any persons professing any particular set of opinions, philosophical, religious, or political; but to the thinking, the candid, and the good of all sects, persuasions, and parties, whosoever and wheresoever they may be. In their hands the writer respectfully leaves it, assured that whatever the judgment of the Public may be as to its matter and argument, his motives will be respected and his attempt unblamed, even by those by whom its failure, if a failure it be, may not be lamented.

It may be proper, in conclusion, to add, that the present volume has in part owed its existence to the attention which an outline of the theory now attempted to be established, given in *Blackwood's Magazine* for March, 1837, under the title of "A Letter to the Right Honourable Lord Brougham," excited at the time of its publication. The author can only hope that the call which was at that time made for his more mature opinions upon the subject, in an enlarged form, may not remain unechoed now that the call is responded to by him; and that the attention which was awarded to the sketch of 1837, may not be refused to the volume of 1841.

Newcastle-upon-Tyne, March 9th, 1841.

CONTENTS.

CHAPTER I.

CHAPTER VII.

CHAPTER VIII.

CHAPTER IX.

CHAPTER X.

CHAPTER XI.

CHAPTER XII.

TRUE LAW OF POPULATION.

CHAPTER I.

A FEW INTRODUCTORY STATEMENTS AND REFLECTIONS.

THE Law of Population is undoubtedly one of the most important questions that can be submitted to human reason. On a cursory or superficial view, it may seem to be the contrary of this. Whilst so much of the earth remains uncultivated and untouched by the hand of man, and whilst that which is so touched is so imperfectly dealt with, it may appear rather a curious than a natural anxiety to sum up the actual or probable numbers of mankind, and still more so to anticipate evils from a superflux of population. To the near and patient inquirer, however, appearances are different.

If it be true that the inhabitants of any country or of all countries tend perpetually by their increase to outstrip their means of subsistence, the evil consequences of such a state of things must, at all times and continually, be felt with more or less of severity; it is of no avail to say that the earth can or will, if properly cultivated, afford ample subsistence for all that have ever yet lived upon its surface. It has not been so cultivated; the increase of food, so far from having been pushed up to those limits which some writers have, and perhaps not improperly, assigned as the highest possible, has in most countries been little better than stationary. The question is, therefore, has the tendency of living beings rapidly to increase been existing through all this foregone period, unchecked by anything but the mere want of corresponding subsistence for those who should be born? If it *has*, then, as it appears to the author, a constant state of suffering, more or less mitigated by various national circumstances, must have existed in all times past, or nearly so. If it has *not* (as the author of this volume affirms it has not), the ONUS is to show what OTHER

PRINCIPLE has operated to check population from time to time, to prove the existence of such a principle, and to point out the times, the places, and the mode of its operation. To establish and explain this principle is the object of the following sheets. The immense importance of the subject may, it is hoped, excuse and help to overcome the dryness of some of the details; nor will the candid reader on a topic at once so mysterious, and hitherto unexplained, suffer himself to be startled or turned aside by the apparent strangeness of the first enunciations of views on this subject, (as the author conceives) nearly altogether new, and of facts certainly brought together and laid before the public in their present form for the first time.

It can hardly be expected of any one writing of matters so abstruse, that he should extract from them other entertainment than such subjects are in themselves calculated to produce. He can only, as a matter of prudent adventure, attempt to place the different points in as clear a light as possible, and with as little waste as may be, of the time and patience of his readers: elucidating where he can, all that is naturally involved or dark, and curtailing where he can, all that is naturally diffuse or voluminous.

It is not necessary, nor would it indeed expedite the purposes of clear arrangement or lucid reasoning, to state in this part of the present work the accidental causes which led the author to the following inquiry; suffice it at present to say, these causes were the result of another inquiry, so far collaterally bearing upon the subject now under discussion, as to throw a sudden light upon its fundamental principles, including as it did, a portion of the proofs of the reality of those principles; nor was the author dissatisfied, but quite the contrary, with the manner in which he was thus accidentally led to the road which he has followed. In matters of reasoning, it is upon the whole better to discover a track accidentally than after search for it; because in the former case the imagination is in abeyance, and unconcerned in the result.

When men eagerly seek for a theory, they are too prone to hope they have found the true one, and it is needless to say that we are too ready to believe that which we earnestly wish. A discovery by accident, on the other hand, comes recommended only by itself; as no credit is sought for sagacity, and no reward for ingenuity expected, fancy, at all events, is not moved to interfere. The pleasure which alone is due to the discovery of truth, is not so liable to be given to that self-love which deceives us into the idea that such discovery is ours as matter of merit, because it has come unsought, and of course unanticipated; such was the case with the contemplation of natural facts which led the author to attempt this exhibition of them, and being so, he trusts the remark is neither irrelevant nor useless.

In order to come in the clearest and fairest manner to the subject of this essay, the author deems the following to be the most advisable course. To state, first, in the tersest and at the same time, most lucid manner he can, the law by which he supposes population to be governed and regulated; next, to prove the existence and operation of this law from such facts as he has collected, which in his opinion tend to demonstrate either or both of these points. The GREAT GENERAL LAW then, which, as it seems, really regulates the increase or decrease both of vegetable and of animal life, is this, that whenever a *species* or *genus* is *endangered*, a corresponding effort is invariably made by nature for its preservation and continuance, by an increase of fecundity or fertility; and that this especially takes place whenever such danger arises from a diminution of proper nourishment or food, so that consequently the state of depletion, or the deplethoric state, is favourable to fertility, and that on the other hand, the plethoric state, or state of repletion, is unfavourable to fertility, in the ratio of the intensity of each state, and this probably throughout nature universally, in the vegetable as well as the animal world; further, that as applied to mankind this law produces the following consequences, and acts thus :—

There is in all societies a constant increase going on amongst that portion of it which is the worst supplied with food ; in short, amongst the poorest.

Amongst those in the state of affluence, and well supplied with food and luxuries, a constant decrease goes on. Amongst those who form the mean or medium between these two opposite states ; that is to say, amongst those who are tolerably well supplied with good food, and not overworked, nor yet idle, population is stationary. Hence it follows that it is upon the *numerical proportion* which these three states bear to each other in any society that increase or decrease upon the whole depends.

In a nation where the affluence is sufficient to

balance, by the decrease which it causes amongst the rich, the increase arising from the poor, population will be stationary. In a nation highly and generally affluent and luxurious, population will decrease and decay. In poor and ill-fed communities, population will increase in the ratio of the poverty, and the consequent deterioration and diminution of the food of a large portion of the members of such communities. This is the real and great law of human population, and to show that it unquestionably is so, must be the aim of the following pages.

In bringing forward the great variety of facts bearing upon this important inquiry, the author will begin with those exhibited by the vegetable kingdom; he will next proceed to the animal creation, wherein the same principle is more distinctly developed, ending with the human world, the numbers composing which he will prove to ebb and flow as one or other of the different states he has described more or less prevails; offering, in conclusion, such general reflections as are necessary completely to elucidate his scheme, and to show not only its wonderful agreement with the state of the world, as it is known to exist and to have existed, but

its admirable unison with the wisdom and goodness of that divine Providence which " saw all
that it had made," and saw that all was "very
good," until marred by the wickedness, the folly,
the error, or the ignorance of man.

CHAPTER II.

THE LAW OF INCREASE AND DECREASE IN THE VEGE-TABLE AND ANIMAL KINGDOMS.

TURNING now to the vegetable kingdom, the author would point to the acknowledged existence of this principle in the theory and practice of all Horticulturists, Gardeners, and others engaged in the raising trees, shrubs, flowers, and vegetables. It is a fact, admitted by all gardeners as well as botanists, that if a tree, plant, or flower, be placed in mould, either naturally or artificially made too rich for it, a plethoric state is produced, and fruitfulness ceases. In trees, the effect of strong manures and over-rich soils is that they run to surperfluous wood, blossom irregularly, and chiefly at the extremities of the outer branches, and almost or entirely cease to bear fruit.

With flowering shrubs and flowers the effect is, first, that the flower becomes double, and loses its power of producing seed; next, it ceases almost even to flower. If the application of the stimulus of manure is carried still further, flowers and plants become diseased in the extreme, and speedily die; thus, by this wise provision of Providence, the transmission of disease (the certain consequence of the highly plethoric state, whether in plants, animals, or in mankind,) is guarded against, and the species shielded from danger on the side of plenty. In order to remedy this state when accidentally produced, Gardeners and Florists are accustomed, by various devices, to produce the opposite or deplethoric state; this they familiarly denominate "giving a check." In other words, they put the species in danger in order to produce a correspondingly determined effort of nature to ensure its perpetuation, and the end is invariably attained. Thus, in order to make fruit trees bear plentifully, Gardeners delay or impede the rising of the sap by cutting rings in the bark round the tree. This to the tree is the production of a state of depletion, and the abundance of fruit is the effort of nature to counteract the danger. The fig, when grown in this climate, is particularly liable to drop its fruit when half matured. This, Gardeners now find, can be prevented by pruning the tree so severely as to give it a check; or, if grown in a pot, by cutting a few inches from its roots all round so as to produce the same effect. The result is, that the tree retains, and carefully matures its fruit.

In like manner, when a gardener wishes to save seed from a gourd or cucumber, he does not give the plant an *extra* quantity of manure or warmth. He does just the contrary: he subjects it to some *hardship* and takes the fruit that is *least* fine looking, foreknowing that it will be filled with seed, whilst the finest fruit are nearly destitute. Upon the same principle, it is a known fact, that after severe and long winters the harvests are correspondingly rapid and abundant. Vines bear most luxuriantly after being severely tried by frost; and grass springs in the same extraordinary manner. After the long and trying winter of 1836-7, when the snow lay upon the ground in the northern counties until June, the spring of grass was so wonderful as to cause several minute experiments by various persons. The result was, that in a single night of twelve hours the blade of grass was ascertained frequently to have advanced full three-quarters of an inch ; and wheat and other grain progressed in a similar manner.

Aware of this beautiful law of preservation, the Florist, when he wishes to ensure the luxuriant flowering of a greenhouse or hothouse shrub or plant, exposes it for a time to the cold. The danger caused by the temperature, too low for the nature of the species of plant, is followed invariably by an effort of nature for its safety, and it flowers luxuriantly ; and if a seed-bearing plant, bears seed accordingly.

There is another curious modification of this law exhibited by the vegetable creation, and this is, that immediately before the death, or the sudden cessation of fruitfulness of a tree or shrub, it is observed generally to bear abundantly. This is remarkably the case with the pear and apple when the roots touch the harsh cold blue clay, or any other soil inimical to the health of the tree. It is a last effort to preserve and per-petuate the species, and is the effect of that state of *depletion* through which the tree passes to sterility and death.

The singularly close analogy which these facts bear to that which can be proved, and indeed is well known to take place with the human female, when fed on insufficient food, or when married too near to the usual period of cessation of fertility, will be more fully adverted to in the proper place. In the meantime, what can be more pleasing than to contemplate this beautiful provision of the Governor of all things, by which fruitfulness is *increased* when the danger arises from insufficient nourishment for the plant or vegetable, and, on the other hand, decreased when the peril springs from a surplusage of what is needful. Thus carefully is the species guarded from extinction by want on one hand, and by implanted disease and vitiated and irregular vegetation on the other — a two-fold distribution of extremes, with a medium of average and moderate fruitfulness between them; that happy mean being disturbed only for a time to ensure as far as possible a return to it.

Turning our attention now to the animal creation, this law will be found to be still more distinctly developed, as well as more generally observed and acted upon.

The practical evidence of the farmer, the grazier, and the breeder of horses, is here corroborated by, and, in its turn, helps to prove, the theories of the Physiologist and Natural Historian; whilst, with the human animal, these theories are again demonstrated, both by the theories and practice of the Physician and Pathologist.

There cannot be a doubt that, with the animal creation—including in that term birds and quadrupeds (of the habits of fish we know little or nothing)—fecundity is totally checked by the plethoric state, when induced, and increased, and rendered doubly certain, by the existence of the deplethoric or lean state; whilst a moderated prolificness is the effect of the state between the two. This is more or less the case even with the most prolific animals. The rabbit and the swine are extraordinary in this respect; yet every schoolboy knows that the doe, or female rabbit, and every farmer and breeder knows that the sow will *not* conceive if fed to a certain height of fatness; and that the number of the progeny is generally in the *ratio* of the *leanness* of the animal. All cattle breeders know the same law to be especially true in the cases of the mare, the cow, and the ewe, with which leanness is indispensable to conception; and upon their knowledge of this truth they invariably act. In the mare this is sometimes evinced in an extraordinary degree. A friend of the author, who, being of the medical profession, is peculiarly observant of all cases of this nature, has assured him that he has known a highly-bred blood mare, which, for a length of time, appeared to be incurably barren, and from which the owner was naturally very desirous to obtain a breed, rendered fertile, and ultimately the dam of a numerous progeny, by being put literally to the plough and cart, fed sparingly, and worked down to a state of extreme leanness and temporary exhaustion, by this unusual employment.

In the sheep, however, this principle of increase or decrease is most nicely developed. It is invariably found that, if over-fed, sterility is the consequence. On the other hand, in accordance with the leanness of the animal, a produce of one, two, or three lambs takes place. Upon their knowledge of this fact the improvers of the breed of this animal are accustomed to act. In order to afford the best chance of a perfect animal, it is believed that a produce of one lamb at a birth is desirable; and this the breeders of sheep contrive to secure by apportioning the food of the ewe to such a nicety, that, avoiding sterility on one hand, and a double or triple birth on the other, a single lamb is almost invariably the offspring of the animal so limited. Of the effect of "condition" upon the fertility of animals, this seems to be one of the strongest of all possible proofs.

The conflicts that take place amongst all wild grazing animals at the time of rutting or breeding are no doubt intended for the same end—to lower their condition to the prolific point.

Upon birds the same state of plethora produces similar defertilising effects. This is well known to be the case with domestic poultry, of which the little familiar French fable of " Une Femme et sa Poule" is an amusing evidence. The good dame, desirous of an increased supply of eggs, crams the poor pullet with double rations of grain. The hen, as well she may, becomes enormously fat *(fort grosse)*, and the consequence is, that not another egg will she lay. With other domesticated fowls, similar causes are known to produce similar effects. Tame pigeons will not increase if pampered with an unlimited quantity of food; and to stop the produce of the pigeon-house it is equally effectual to cram them with victuals, or to deny it altogether; in which latter case, inexpert in the art of catering or feeding, they are compelled to wander so long and far in search of it, and are altogether so ignorant of their duty, that they cannot supply

their young ones; in the former they have none
to supply.

Upon the whole, there can hardly be a doubt
that, as far as the vegetable creation and the
lower animals are concerned, the rule is palpable
and invariable that over-manuring and over-
feeding check increase ; whilst, on the other hand,
a limited or deficient nutriment stimulates and
adds to it. In support of the truth of this law
we have the united testimony of the cultivators
of the ground, of all grades and descriptions,
and of the numerous persons who make it the
business of their lives to superintend the breeding
of animals. The facts supported by these testimonies do not appear in books, nor are much
regarded, save by those whose livelihood depends
upon their knowledge of them. They are,
however, confirmed to be truths by a series
of experience, sufficient to establish anything
capable of being demonstrated by evidence.
That they have not been thought to be of that
value which they really are, is not extraordinary.
The persons cognizant of them never dreamed
of reasoning further, not having the slightest
idea of the existence of any controversy upon
which such facts might be supposed to
be capable of throwing light. The long state

of abeyance as matter of reasoning, and as part of the foundations upon which conclusions more important were to be built, in which they have been held, does not however detract from their value. Many estimable things have been tossed about as rubbish for centuries, before their real bearings were discovered ; and such has been the fate of these—no uncommon fate.

CHAPTER III.

THE LAW OF INCREASE AND DECREASE OF THE RACE OF MANKIND.

THAT the law of Increase or Decrease as above described, is that which acts throughout the vegetable creation, as well as the world of inferior animals, up to man, as the regulator of the numbers of the different species, the author thinks he has shown abundant reasons for supposing. This supposition, however, is not meant by any means to shut out, nor does it at all necessarily shut out the truth of that assertion which affirms that to different species of animals or plants different *capabilities* of increase are assigned by Nature. The quantity of seed borne by one plant differs naturally from that borne by another, under the most favourable circumstances. The power of increase in some kinds of fish is calculated to be far beyond that of any other animal or vegetable production of Nature. Birds and beasts of prey seem especially also to be more strictly limited by Nature in their powers of increasing their numbers, than those which feed, either in part or altogether, upon vegetables; for which more than one probable reason shall be assigned in the proper place. All that is meant is, that, be the range of the natural power to increase in any species what it may, the *plethoric* state invariably checks it, and the *deplethoric* state invariably developes it; and that this happens in the exact *ratio* of the intensity and completeness of each state, until each state be carried so far as to bring about the actual death of the animal or plant itself.

This law, then, being the regulator of the numbers of all living or semi-living creatures, up to man himself, we now come to the great question of all, viz.:—whether this analogy is continued; and whether the race of mankind is subject to the same law of fertility with the rest of that creation at the head of which he seems to stand? The author is well aware of one objection, plausible indeed, but the reverse. of solid, which will here be urged against him, and it may as well be stated at once, and disposed of,

" What folly is it (will the objector exclaim)
to place animals acting on instinct merely, and
destitute of mind, properly so called, upon a
level with rational man, or to imagine there can
be any such analogy as this between creatures so
totally dissimilar, and so far removed from each
other ? " " Reason (it will be said) was given to
man for the very purpose of checking and control-
ling his propensities and passions ; and yet this is
to be set at nothing—thrown out of the question.—a merely gross and animal check substi-
tuted for that of the ' *mens divinior ;* ' and men
and women are to be fattened into sterility, or
starved into fruitfulness, like the stock upon a
farm !"

Now, in reply to this, it is to be observed,
that it is not here denied that reason was given
to mankind as a " check" and " control" upon
their passions, amongst other things. There is
not the slightest intention to deny this directly
or indirectly, provided the proper and obvious
meaning of the term " check" be adhered to.
What, then, is the meaning of this verb-active
" to check" or to " control ?" It is the power
to withstand an impulse—to hold it in a modified
dominion—to regulate its direction and extent
of course, as contradistinguished from the power

to eradicate, to destroy, or totally to keep down or neutralize. This is the meaning of " check" or " control ;" and doubtless men's reason may, and does, in all cases, more or less, exercise this power over their passions. No man, however hungry, satisfies his soul at another's board, save by invitation ; no man, however thirsty, ever drinks at another's spring without leave given. But this is the regulation, not the extinction of passions co-existent with human nature itself.

That the intercourse between the sexes must, in all civilized states of society, be regulated and bound down in various ways, is indisputable and undisputed. But still this is regulation, and not extinction. To be the husband of one wife is a precept salutary in itself ; and which, in a state of imperfect civilization, is violated more in appearance than reality. It is a precept which religion teaches, nature encourages, and common sense ratifies. To modify further would be to extinguish, not to regulate ; and against this Nature rises at once in arms, and has decreed that such attempts shall be as vain in effect as they are foolish in imagination.

There is every reason to believe that, by a special provision of nature, all attempts to limit the number of children, by delaying to middle-life the period of marriage, are vain and futile ; inasmuch as the rapidity of conception, at all events, amongst those classes whose manner of living presents no bar to fertility, may be shown to *increase* in the proportion of the *lateness of the time* when marriage has taken place.

This shall be proved in the course of this essay ; in the meantime, the author trusts that he has drawn a distinction which no reader can fail to recognise : viz., that regulation is one thing, extinction, or total denial, another ; that reason is competent to the first, but eschews the second, as a task not to be achieved, and an attempt at domination, against which Nature must ever revolt, and which no sophistry, however subtle, can render for a moment palatable to the commonest, as well as best feelings of mankind. Having thus cleared the ground of these matters of objection, such as they are, it now remains to go at once into the important part of this treatise, into the pith and marrow of this " great argument," and to show that the law of population here described applies itself also to mankind, and regulates the numbers of human, as it does that of other created beings.

The best method, as it appears to the author, to effect this, in a manner the most clear and distinct, will be, first, to give those general, but striking instances of the existence of this law, which are to be observed in the general history of mankind, ancient and modern. Next, to demonstrate it by reference to limited bodies of men, as to whose exact history and circumstances we have accurate knowledge; and then to prove that it is borne out by the actual differences in the condition of nations existing at this day, as shown in the best statistical accounts of that condition.

Thus, we shall first trace those general and striking lights which historical annals chance to afford, and which are the more valuable because they are wholly accidental.

Next, we shall see these general views accurately borne out by more minute accounts of small bodies of men, the requisite minutiæ of whose history we have in our power; and these proofs again we shall find to be remarkably corroborated by the actual state of the nations of the world, as at present known—a body of evidence so varied in detail, and so overpoweringly tending in one direction, as to constitute little short of positive or direct demonstration.

One of the oldest traditions of facts, bearing evidence of the truth of this Law of Population, is undoubtedly that which attributes a remarkable

fecundity to the " Icthyophagi," or those nations
who lived chiefly upon fish. That this tradition
has existed time immemorial, is quite undoubted,
and upon it is built the mythological fiction of
Venus being sprung from the Sea. Strange mix-
ture of fancy with truth ; to the latter of which,
however, Aristotle bears testimony ; and which,
in point of fact, is admitted, and attempted to
be accounted for by political economists of the
present day. That a fish-diet is the cause of
unusual prolificness no one can doubt, who
knows anything of the Highlands and Western
Islands of Scotland, where the food of the inhabitants is, in a great measure, derived from the
Sea ; where even the eggs of sea-fowls are not
eaten, but made an article of traffic ; and where
the only animal food tasted by the poorer natives
is an occasional " braxie," or sheep, which has
died of the rot ? Amongst these poor people, a
family of from ten to twenty children is by no
means an uncommon occurrence, but the contrary ; and instances of females who have borne
above twenty children are far from rare.

To suppose that a fish-diet is peculiarly the
cause of this is absurd ; because, in Ireland, where
the diet is vegetable chiefly, and that vegetable
the light and watery potato, the same results

occur. It is notorious that from the Sister Island, as that country is quaintly termed, the great bulk of the cattle and stock of all kinds is exported, either alive or as salted provisions. It is notorious that such wheat as there is grown shares the same fate, and that the bulk of the people rarely even taste the luxury of a bit of bacon ; and that their exclusive food is the potato, with such supplies of fish as their seas and lakes afford them. The consequence of this is, that this beautiful grazing country, by nature intended to be pastoral, and which like other pastoral countries would have been thinly peopled had the population been permitted by their landlords to live upon the produce of their own green and rich fields, is over-populated to extent only inferior to that to which China and India are so, where also the use of animal food is equally almost unknown, and where emigration is less frequent. It can indeed hardly be doubted that, but for the continual emigration from Ireland and the Highlands of Scotland, which is perpetually going on, the populousness of these countries would, at no remote period, equal that of India or even China, overflowing with human beings as this last named immense district has doubtless been for many ages.

It may probably here be objected by many readers that this is all "gratuitous assertion;" that the facts of the populousness of Ireland, the Scotch Highlands, India, and China, may be incontrovertible. That it may be equally undoubted that the food of these countries is vegetable. Still, it will be demanded, where is the proof that this fecundity is the effect of the poverty and scarcity of the food of the inhabitants? — that the child-murders of China, the famines amongst the millions of India, and Ireland, and the Hebrides, are the ultimate effects of rice and potatoes?

To this there is a general as well as a particular answer; and the general answer should first be given. That answer is a general appeal to the admissions of all medical and physiological authorities of modern, and many of ancient times, that such diet has, in fact, the prolific tendency here ascribed to it ; and a general appeal to existing populations, which are universally found *thin* in pastoral countries, where the food is animal food chiefly ; *denser*, where it is mixed partly with vegetable aliment ; *denser still*, where it is vegetable only, but with plenty ; *densest of all*, where it is vegetable, but with scarcity superadded.

The evidence of medical men is now unanimous as to the effect of the plethoric state in checking fecundity in the human female, both by preventing conception and occasioning miscarriage ; but of the opposite effects produced by a poorer and lower diet, the proofs are commonly known to be perpetual. Dr. Cheyne, and the older dietetic writers all notice these facts ; but the accumulative evidence is now considered by medical persons as irresistible.

There are numerous instances where the occurrence of misfortune, and consequent privations, have given families to those who were childless in their prosperity ; and, as elucidating the same law, we may adduce another fact, well known to medical persons, which is the extraordinary tendencies to propagation evinced by both sexes when semi-convalescent, after enfeebling and attenuating epidemics, such as fevers, pestilences and plagues ; and the consequent extraordinary rapidity with which population recovers itself in those countries where the plague, the marsh fever, or famines, which cause many of these epidemics, have made havoc.

A general glance at the map of the world, with a general statistical account, will show results corresponding with this law. Thus, in Russia, where butcher's-meat is a drug,

and vegetable food a luxury, the numbers to
to the square league are trifling.

In Poland, France, Italy, and the Low Countries, where the diet is mixed, but plentiful,
population is moderately dense.

In India, in Ireland, and in China, where no
animal food almost is eaten, the population is
excessively dense, and constant pauperism and
periodical famines form decided features in the
history of these countries.

It is not, however, by mere general views like
these that this nice and most important question
can be decided; it must be made minutely and
particularly the subject of examination; it must
be shown to be true as regards countries and
their population, taking each separately, country
by country.

Where different provinces of the same country
differ from each other as to population, it must
be shown to be in accordance with this law.
Where different bodies of men in the same community retrograde, are stationary, or increase in
numbers, the same must be proved with regard
to such bodies; for it is only by being borne out
and proved to be true, under all these various
modifications of society, that the existence of a

law, which is not only general but invariable, can be satisfactorily proved and demonstrated. To commence this proof shall be the business of the next chapter.

CHAPTER IV.

THE LAW OF INCREASE AND DECREASE, AS AMONGST LIMITED BODIES OF MEN, EXEMPLIFIED.

Looking at bodies of men, one of the most striking facts of all history is the decay to which all systems of nobility, however widely extended these privileges may have been, seem to be subjected. " Old families (says that most erudite and curious of all observers, Sir Thomas Browne, in his ' Hydriotaphia') last not *three oaks!*" Nothing can be more true.

Let us take as an instance the Peers and Baronets of Great Britain, and nothing can be more striking than the perpetual decay of a body of. men, who, possessing large estates and privileges of the most enviable nature, have had apparently every means as well as every motive to transmit these desirable possessions to lineal heirs. The pride of name, the pride of dominion, the pride of power, all seem to secure the certainty of such transmission ; and yet what has been the reality ? This it has been—that the Peerage of England, instead of being old, is recent, and the Baronetage, though comparatively of modern origin, equally so. In short, that few, if any, of the Norman nobility, and almost as few of the original baronets' families of King James the First, exist at this moment ; and that, but for perpetual creations, both orders must have been all but extinct. The following table shows that the great majority of the House of Peers has been created since the year 1760, that is to say, within eighty years of the present time, and since the commencement of the reign of George the Third, whose accession was in the October of that year ; a period within the memory of many now living :—

The number of Peers in 1837.		Number created since 1760.	
Dukes . .	21 . .	. .	5 Dukes
Marquises .	19 . .	. .	18 Marquises
Earls . .	108 . .	. .	58 ·Earls
Viscounts .	17 . .	. .	13 Viscounts
Barons . .	185 . .	. .	153 Barons
	350		247
Scottish Peers	16 ⎱ . .	. .	25
Irish Peers .	28 ⎰		
Total . .	394		272 Total since 1760.

Thus it appears that, within the memory of man, 272 of the 394 Peers of Parliament in 1837, have been created. The decay of the order of Baronets has been, perhaps, still more rapid and extraordinary. The order itself was commenced only in 1611, by King James the First, as a means of raising money, principally for the Irish War of that period.

It was suggested as a cheap mode of raising supplies, by the celebrated Lord Bacon, one of whose name was in the original Baronetage, and is one of the few of those originally created, whose descendants remain. The sum paid for this honour was very large, and it is therefore certain that the earlier Baronets were all wealthy men and of great estate. The results are as follows :—

Since the creation of the order of Baronets, in 1611, seven hundred and fifty-three Baronetcies have become extinct. In short, the number of extinct Baronets are more, *in toto*, than the existing Baronets, up to the year 1819, when the Baronets were six hundred and thirty-five only.

From 1611 to 1819, one hundred and thirty-nine Baronets had been raised to the Peerage, and thus taken out of the list of Baronets. Still, supposing all these Peerages to be now existing, which is not the case, this would only make the whole number, including those made Peers, seven hundred and seventy-four; that is to say, the living Baronets and Baronet Peers would, in that case, only exceed the extinct Baronets by *twenty-one!* Thus it is evident, that but for perpetual new creations, we should hardly have had a Baronet existing. Of James the First's creation, in A. D. 1611, only *thirteen* families now remain. Of all he created up to 1625, the year of his death, *thirty-nine* only remain; a decay certainly extraordinary, and not to be accounted for upon the ordinary ideas of mortality and power of increase amongst mankind.

The author is not unaware that in the cases above quoted, there arise out of the nature of the institutions themselves, causes of extinction which do not apply to a population, or to society in general. A single failure of offspring makes a gap in *the body*, whilst even *extra* fecundity in another quarter is only allowed to keep up *the line*. For instance, Lord S., or Sir John S., dies childless: Lord R., or Sir John R., supplies a dozen or fourteen descendants. One would have sufficed to fill the place, and we cannot make use of the surplus to supply other deficiencies. This is clearly enough one cause of the extinction of titles, which, where there are many sons, is conferred upon one alone, but which is lost in case of failure of heirs. But this one cause will not account for the rapid and perpetual decay of nobility as exhibited, not only in the English Peerage and Baronetage, but amongst the nobility and higher orders of other countries, both ancient and modern, where the cause above alluded to does not exist.

We have the testimony of Addison (who quotes Amelot) as to the extraordinary decrease of the Venetian nobility, although *all* the sons are ennobled by birth. Chastellux and Heylin say the same of the French and Netherlandish Noblesse. Mr. Malthus himself, also bears witness to the strange decrease of the bourgeoisie, or wealthy class of the town of Berne; although the fact is strongly opposed to his preconceived opinions. Addison's remarks, as repeated in the work of the late Michael Thomas Sadler on this subject, are as follows. " Amelot reckoned in his time 2500 nobles that had voices in the Council; but at present I am told there are not at most 1500, notwithstanding the addition of many new families since that time. It is *very strange,* that with this advantage they are not able to keep up their numbers, *considering that the nobility spreads equally through all the brothers,* and that so *very few* are destroyed by the wars of the Republic."

Mr. Malthus, at page 278 of his "Essay on Population," gives the following statement as to the town of Berne.   "From the year 1583 to 1654, the Sovereign Council admitted into the bourgeoisie 487 families, of which 379 became extinct in the space of two centuries, and in 1783, only 108 of them remained!   During the *hundred* years from 1684 to 1784, *two hundred and seven* Bernoise families became extinct. From 1624 to 1712, the bourgeoisie was given to eighty families; in 1623, the Sovereign Council united the numbers of one hundred and twelve different families, of which *fifty-eight* only remain."   From these facts, it is apparent that the law of decrease is not only active amongst those included under the title of nobility, but amongst any class of men, however entitled, to whom the means of full and generous living are not denied; the bourgeoisie of the comparatively poor and republican town of Berne being no more proof against it than the high-blooded nobles of Italy and France.   The evidence of Tacitus, however, as to the certain and wonderful activity of this principle of decay, amongst those to whom is allotted the pride of place, is perhaps the most extraordinary. Under the Emperor Claudius, it seems to have been necessary, by an admission of the best families, who were not actually patrician, to renovate this powerful class; and this is the historian's brief but most instructive account of this matter. " Jisdem diebus in numerum Patriciorum adscivit Cæsar vetustissimum quemque e Senatu, aut quibus clari parentes fuerant. Paucis jam reliquis familiarum quas Romulus Majorum, et Lucius Brutus Minorum Gentium, ad pellaverat : exhaustis etiam quas Dictator Cæsar Lege Cassia, et Princeps Augustus Lege Sænia, sublegere."—*Annal*: lib. xi. cap. xxv.

" About the same time Claudius enrolled in the Patrician order such of the ancient senators as stood recommended by their illustrious birth and the merit of their ancestors. The line of those families which were styled by Romulus ' the first class of nobility,' and by Brutus ' the second,' was almost extinct. Even those of more recent date, created in the time of Julius Cæsar by the Cassian law, and under Augustus by the

Sænian, were well nigh exhausted."—*Murphy's Translation.*

In his translation of this extraordinary account, Murphy has softened the directness of Tacitus. There is nothing in the original to answer to the words "*well nigh* exhausted" in the last sentence. Tacitus says, in plain terms, that "even the Patrician families created by the Dictator Cæsar, and by Augustus, *were* exhausted;" meaning of course, not *extinct absolutely*, but exhausted for all the purposes for which they were created into a class. This is an instance of Patrician decay exceeding those of modern times.

That the nobility of Romulus and Brutus should in Claudius Cæsar's time have been worn out, is hardly to be wondered at; but that the new creations of the Dictator Julius, and his nephew Augustus, should also have perished, is a striking event. Supposing even their numbers comparatively few, it is still a startling fact, that in *less than a century* few of these families should remain. Yet such is Tacitus' assertion; for, between the assumption of Dictatorship by Julius Cæsar and this period of the reign of Claudius, ninety-two years only elapsed.

The instances already quoted will have given

the reader reason to think that, not only amongst those classes of men styled nobility, but even amongst classes not ennobled by name, but enabled by fortune to imitate the full and luxurious habits of noblemen, the law of decrease is strongly developed. This law of plethoric decrease, however, does not stop here. As it descends, it certainly mitigates. What was plague under the Line and between the Tropics, becomes malignant fever in more temperate climates; mitigates again into typhus as the cold increases, and disappears altogether beyond the Arctic and Antarctic Circles. Such is precisely the course of the principle of decrease. As men become lower in circumstances it diminishes; lower again, it becomes nothing, until *privation* comes, and then *the opposite principle* immediately appears, and goes on growing in intensity, in the ratio of privation and consequent depletion and debility, in all their varied forms of weakened and attenuated constitutions.

As a proof of the prevalence of this principle of decrease amongst a class of men, lower in society than those already mentioned, but still well able by circumstances to induce the plethoric or non-increasing state of constitution, the author will now adduce some facts derived from the archives of a more humble *privileged class of men—the free burgesses* of certain rich and exclusive boroughs. The first example he will take from the rich and ancient borough, within the precincts of which he is now writing, and of whose corporate governing body he was recently a member. He will instance the free burgesses of Newcastle-upon-Tyne. In doing this it is, in commencement, proper to state that the corporation of Newcastle-upon-Tyne is, and has been for centuries, one of the richest incorporations of this or any other country. Of this wealth its burgesses of all ranks have, more or less, shared the benefits. Up to about the year 1760, the freemen or free burgesses enjoyed a complete and close monopoly of the trade of the town of Newcastle. With the exception of a small space called "the Castle-yard, or Garth," which, by a fiction of law, is supposed to be part and parcel of the neighbouring county of Northumberland, in order that the county assizes may be held there, no person, not free of the borough, was permitted to open a shop within its boundaries or liberties. Free artizans also exclusively enjoyed the privilege of being employed, at liberal wages, in all the operative business of this wealthy corporation. There were, and are, well-endowed hospitals for decayed freemen or their widows. They possessed the depasturage of extensive and fine grazing grounds of many hundreds of acres. They had a complete monopoly of the carriage of goods from the quay, which was vested in an incorporate company of "Free Porters," who were paid extravagant rates of carriage. As they enjoyed the exclusive privilege of electing members of Parliament, they also had a sort of patent for all local government-offices, for which members of Parliament recommend candidates. There is also an endowment for lending young tradesmen money, on bonded security, to assist their business, the benefits which they enjoyed exclusively ; and lastly, they were constant and welcome guests at all treats, feasts, and entertainments given at a Mansion House, kept always open for such visitors, at an enormous expense.

Beyond all this, they had beneficial grants of quays for the deposit of ballast, from which both the corporation and the depositors reaped handsome revenues, and the maritime part of their population also derived solid advantages from an endowed establishment called the Trinity House, where an endowed school for maritime purposes is provided. There are also other endowed schools for general education, gratis, for the children of free burgesses.

Surrounded with such advantages, it required

an unusual strain of imprudence indeed to prevent a Newcastle free burgess from doing well in
worldly matters; and the body as a consequence
were generally wealthy men in their different
stations in society. That these enviable distinc-
tions were carefully guarded from competitors
need not be doubted. The freedom of the town
was never sold, nor ever given, except as an
honour to some few distinguished or illustrious
strangers. There were only two ways of acquiring the franchise, viz., by inheritance or by
servitude. *Every son of a free burgess was free;*
but if the father had not paid the necessary fees,
and formally assumed the franchise, this barred
the son, although the grandfather had been free.
The servitude was a *bona fide* apprenticeship to a
freeman of *seven* years; and this was most
scrupulously insisted upon.

Under all these favourable circumstances, *all
the sons of a free burgess being free,* it might be
expected that they should go on rapidly increasing
their numbers. With them the usual bar to
marriage, poverty, was out of the question; and
their monopoly of trade directly encouraged an
early settlement in life. The contrary, however,
has indubitably been the case; up to the time
when they lost their trading monopoly, they seem
hardly to have maintained their numbers; and

there is good reason for supposing they might even have decreased, had it not been for the aid of those who became free by servitude; which last seem to have probably *exceeded* in number those who acquired it by inheritance.

Since the loss of their exclusive privileges as to trade, the increase has been unquestionably greater; but the whole history of this body of men exemplifies, in a very extraordinary manner, the difficulty with which a well-fed community maintains its numerical strength.

The first table is a statement of the numbers of claimants of the franchise for five years, distinguishing the claimants by *birth* from those by *servitude*. The latter, it will be seen, still predominate. The next table is the polls of all the contested elections from A. D. 1710, inclusive, up to the passing of the Reform Bill in 1832. This table proves that the number of freemen at the period of the great contest of A. D. 1722 was nearly the same as the number existing at the periods of the subsequent contests, in 1841, 1774, 1777, and 1780. These tables are certainly correct, and were kindly extracted and calculated from the books of the Stewards of the Incorporated Companies by their excellent Secretary, John Brown, Esq., at the request of the Author.

TABLE I.

CLAIMED THE FREEDOM OF NEWCASTLE-UPON-TYNE.

Years.	By Birth.	By Servitude.	Total.
1832	43 Claimed.	83 Claimed.	
1833	40 . .	57 . .	
1834	47 . .	63 . .	
1835	86 . .	88 . .	
1836	31 . .	59 . .	
	247	350	597 Claimants.

Of this table Mr. Brown remarks—" 311 persons only were *admitted*. I do not know the proportion of the parties admitted by birth or servitude, but conclude they are in the same ratio as the claimants." Thus, then, it is probable that the additions to the burgess-roll by servitude *have more than kept pace* with those by birth. The principal cause of the non-admissions is unwillingness, or else inability, to pay the fees. These amount to a heavy sum for a young man in narrow circumstances. This obstacle, however, generally disappears before contested elections, when those whose claims are valid become all at once possessed of the means of assuming the franchise, or, as it is called, " taking up their freedom !"

TABLE II.

NUMBERS OF VOTES POLLED AT THE CONTESTED ELECTIONS FOR
NEWCASTLE-UPON-TYNE.

Years.	Votes.		
1710	Sir William Blackett	1177	Two days only. 1700 voters probably.
	Mr. Wrightsen	886	
	Mr. W. Carr	609	
1715	Sir William Blackett	639	No time given.
	Mr. Wrightsen	550	
	Mr. Clavering	263	
1722	Mr. W. Carr	1234	2000 voters probably.
	Sir William Blackett	1158	
	Mr. Wrightsen	831	
1727	Sir William Blackett	1202	Three days. 2000 voters probably.
	Mr. N. Fenwick	1189	
	Mr. Carr	620	
1734	Mr. Walter Blackett	1354	Eight days. 1795 voters.
	Mr. N. Fenwick	1083	
	Mr. W. Carr	716	
1741	Sir Walter Blackett	1453	A great contest. Six days. 2391 voters.
	Mr. N. Fenwick	1231	
	Mr. Matthew Ridley	1131	
	Mr. Wm. Carr	683	
1774	Sir Walter Blackett	1432	A great contest. 2162 voters.
	Sir Matthew Ridley	1411	
	Captain Phipps	795	
	Mr. Delaval	677	
1777	Sir John Trevelyan	1163	2231 voters.
	A. R. Stoney Bowes	1068	
1780	Sir Matthew Ridley	1408	2245 voters.
	A. R. Stoney Bowes	1135	
	Mr. Delaval	1085	
1820	Sir Matthew Ridley	particulars wanting.	A single day. 800 voters.
	Mr. Ellison		
	Hon. Mr. Scott		

In 1832, the number of freemen resident within seven miles of Newcastle was 1619 only.—(*Mr. Brown's note.*)

From these results it is evident that, although
it is certain that the population of Newcastle-
upon-Tyne has been steadily, and of late even
rapidly increasing, as may be proved by the
results of the different enumerations, as well as
by the greatly augmented amount of Custom-
house receipts; yet the freemen, or free-burgesses,
despite the aid of those acquiring freedom by
servitude, have not materially helped that increase.

It also singularly coincides with the law of
increase here attempted to be demonstrated, that
such material increase of numbers as has taken
place in the body of free-burgesses, has occurred
since the loss of their exclusive trading privileges,
and the consequent diminution of the fulness of
their means of living, by an influx of active competitors.

The positive conclusions which the author has
drawn from the foregoing results, he has not
drawn without being well aware that they are
liable to certain objections; inasmuch as, besides
probable modes of living, there are other accidental circumstances likely to diminish and keep
down the number upon the burgess roll, and to
affect in other ways the validity of the strong
conclusions come to. These objections he cannot

state better than by quoting the statement of
them made to him by one most eminently qualified to inquire into such evidence, that is to say,
the talented Town Clerk of the Borough, John
Clayton, Esq., who was at the kind pains to
consider and sift much of that portion of the
documentary testimony upon which this theory
is founded. The following are Mr. Clayton's
remarks as to this portion of the argument : --

" Newcastle, Sept. 3, 1837.

" The conclusions which you draw from the
" past and present state of the body of freemen
" are open to some observations. I believe it to
" be quite true, that during the last century there
" was very little increase in the number of that
" privileged class. But it must be borne in mind,
" that during the same period the freemen were
" subjected to the severe check of the loss of
" their privilege of exclusive trading, and became
" a minority of the inhabitants of the town, in-
" stead of being, as they were at the commence-
" ment of the last century, almost its sole
" inhabitants. It will be found, I think, also,
" that the town itself was not nearly so much
" extended during the whole of last century, as
" it has been during thirty-six years of this.

" In the year 1734, the whole number of free-
" men polled at a contest, which drew together
" the non-resident as well as the resident freemen,
" did not exceed *eighteen hundred*. At present,
" (1837) the number of registered freemen, resi-
" dent within seven miles of the borough, exceeds
" eighteen hundred; and the non-resident, I
" calculate, may be nearly equal in number.
" There are also circumstances to be considered
" which prevent this class having the full benefit
" of the fecundity of the species. In the first
" place, females and their descendants do not
" assist us in keeping up *our* number (I speak in
" the first person, as one of the body); and in
" the next place, the rule (correctly stated in
" your letter) by which the franchise is lost to
" the children if the father omits the ceremony
" of admission, operates very greatly as a check
" to our increase. I will put a case, within my
" knowledge, and not an extreme case, which
" will show the practical working of this rule.
" A.B., a freeman, dies, leaving three sons. The
" eldest remains in this country and dies, leaving
" an only son, whom we retain as a freeman.
" The two younger sons do not take up their
" freedom at all. One of them goes abroad and
" dies, leaving five sons. The other enters the

" army, and finally settles in a distant part of
" the country, where he leaves four sons. Thus,
" if we had the full benefit of the *natural* increase
" of the species, we should have had *ten* freemen
" in the place of A. B., the grandfather. Now,
" through the operation of our artificial restric-
" tion, we have only *one!* According to the
" statement supplied to you, which I believe to
" be correct, our gain by apprenticeship is
" counterbalanced by the loss we suffer from
" inability or disinclination of claimants to take
" up the freedom, notwithstanding the generous
" aid afforded them by candidates for their suf-
" frages at elections."

The objections which are embodied in these, at
first sight striking and apposite comments, seem
to the author to admit of satisfactory solution.
That the loss of the female line must affect the
actual numbers of the class of free burgesses most
materially, is evident enough. In short, the probable loss must be nearly one half; inasmuch as
in an extended population the number of females
born nearly equals that of males. But this effect
upon actual number has nothing to do with *ratio
of increase.* There is no reason adduced for supposing that if the franchise had been conferred

upon females also, and their descendants, and if
such females, by marrying, conferred upon their
husbands and families the same advantages and
fruits of privilege and property, which freemen do
upon their wives and families, that their fecundity would have been greater, or at all different,
their circumstances of living being supposed to
be the same.

If increase there was, then the *ratio* would
have been *the same*, though the *numbers* would
have been *greater*. The start would indeed be
made with *double the number ;* but there is
nothing to show why the *ratio of prolificness*
should be increased. That objection which accounts for the want of increase, by supposing
that the loss caused by omission to take up the
franchise counterbalances the gain arising from
admissions earned by servitude, is less easy to
parry. That much loss may be and often is so
caused, cannot be denied. The answer is, that
upon the whole statement this loss is evidently
insufficient to account for *the whole failure* of
increase, though it may account for *part of it*.

It is shown on all the statements, that during
the early part of the last century the increase
was trifling, and that after the loss of the trading
monopoly about 1760, up to the present time, the

increase has been more. Now had omission of
taking up freedom been the check, the direct
contrary must have been the case, because the
means of paying the fees must have been diminished—first by the lessened means ; next, by the
want of contested elections, of which there were
none from 1780 up to 1832, save the two days
of 1820, and because the motives for emigrating
must have increased ; and therefore *this* check
of omission must have been rendered *more stringent*, and of augmented efficacy after 1760. The
event of the admitted increase *since* 1760, however, contradicts this ; and it follows that there
must have been *some* OTHER CHECK *removed of
more efficacy than the omission to claim;* inasmuch
as the effect of *its removal* has been totally to
overcome and neutralize the increased stringency
of the other, as is proved by the growth of the
burgess population during the last named period.
The cause of that effect, the author asserts, was
the *poverty* created by the loss of the exclusive
privileges ; the " severe check" to the prosperity
having an inverted effect upon the prolificness of
the burgesses ; or, in other words, the check to the
prolificness of the burgesses ; or, in other words,
the check to the accumulation of wealth, being
the removal of a check, or rather a positive

stimulus to increased population. In order, however, to put this probable truth in a still clearer and more indisputable point of view, the author will instance the facts as to the increase of another body of freemen, obtaining their franchise in the same way as those of Newcastle-upon-Tyne, but not possessed of lucrative privileges like those of the latter—the burgesses of Berwick-upon-Tweed.

These facts were obtained through the instrumentality of the kind friend, whose assistance has been already alluded to, and they may be entirely depended upon. The freedom of the borough of Berwick, it has already been remarked, is obtained upon the same conditions, or as nearly so as possible, as those upon which depends the franchise of Newcastle, inheritance or servitude. The property and emoluments of the Mayor and Burgesses derived from the incorporation are trifling, however; and the freemen of Berwick, compared with those of Newcastle, are a comparatively poor class of men.

Here, then, are two bodies of men, selected in the same manner, under the same artificial circumstances, differing only in point of wealth and endowments. Amongst these men the inability to take up the freedom must be as great as amongst the Newcastle claimants, because they are less wealthy.

The indifference about it must be greater, because it confers no lucrative privileges, except as far as the sale of votes for Members of Parliament may be occasionally lucrative to the corrupt voter. The tendency to emigrate must also be fully equal to the tendency in the former place. Yet what is the result, on a comparison of facts? That the free burgesses of Berwick have increased during the last century in a ratio far beyond that of the increase of the Newcastle free burgesses, an effect only to be accounted for in the fact of their greater comparative poverty. The results for the last century, and the ratio of claims by birth or servitude, are as follow :—

TABLE I.

NUMBER OF CLAIMANTS OF THE FRANCHISE OF BERWICK-ON-TWEED.

From 1829 to 1836	By Birth.	Servitude.	Admitted by Ticket.	Total.
	123	29	5	157

TABLE II.

COMPARATIVE NUMBERS OF FREEMEN AFTER A CENTURY.

Year.	No. of Burgesses.	
1737	583	No division into resident and non-resident.
1837	1,116	Of these 450 were resident, 666 non-resident.

TABLE III.

NUMBERS POLLED IN RECENT ELECTIONS.

1831	..	..	366 polled (before the Reform Bill).
1837	..	.	393 polled (after the Reform Bill).

Thus it appears that the freemen of Berwick-upon-Tweed have all but doubled their number in the course of the last hundred years, from 1737 to 1837 ; that the tendency to emigrate is greater here than in Newcastle, inasmuch as the non-residents much exceed the residents in 1837 ; and lastly, that during the last six years their numbers must have increased considerably, inasmuch as some of the 366 polled in 1831 were probably non-residents ; whereas, all the 393 polled in 1837 must have been residents within seven miles.

If we extend our examination to other corporate bodies in various parts of the kingdom, the same tendency to diminution and decay of the numbers of the privileged classes, seems, more or less, to pervade them all. The various ways in which the franchise descends, or is acquired, of course varies the results ; but the general bearing and tendency are one and the same. Thus, in the City of Durham the freedom is acquired by apprenticeship, in the same manner as it is in Newcastle-upon-Tyne and in Berwick-upon-Tweed, but the hereditary descent is more limited. The franchise is enjoyed only by the eldest son of a free burgess of Durham, save and except in the United Company of Grocers and Mercers, where all the sons inherit. This company being composed generally of men with some capital, if the theory now advocated be true, would certainly require some extra aid to keep their guildry in existence, and this it appears they have required. The result of an inquiry into the numbers of the freemen of Durham, shows that for some generations a diminution has been for the most part going on, though the admissions by servitude are numerous. The diminution of their numbers has, however, been less than the limitation of the inheritance would have led a hasty inquirer to expect. When we find, however, as is the case, that the mass of the free burgesses here are generally much poorer than are those of the boroughs already alluded to, the apparent anomaly is accounted for.

In the year 1678, was the first election for Members of Parliament for this city, when *eight hundred and thirty-eight voters polled.* Between this time and 1761, there was probably a small decrease in their number, for though *one thousand and fifty persons voted as freemen*, yet *two hundred and sixty-four* of these were created for the occasion, under a bye-law afterwards set aside. This reduces the actual number of free burgesses to *seven hundred and eighty-eight*, a diminution of the numbers in the election of 1678. In the year 1802 (a violent contest), a small increase seems to have existed, as *nine hundred and eighty-two* are stated to have polled. Since then they have decreased, the number resident within seven miles at this time (1841) being calculated at *four hundred and fifty only ;* the probable non-residents are about *two hundred.* What is a very striking fact, is, that the United Mercers and Grocers Company, in which alone ALL THE SONS inherit the franchise, comprises only THIRTEEN individuals, the numbers being kept up by the poorer companies. The average of admissions to the franchise of late years is twenty-nine. Thus, in fifteen years, a number equal to the present total number of resident burgesses has been admitted ; and yet the numbers, on the whole, decrease.

In the borough of Richmond in Yorkshire, the franchise descends, as at Durham, through the eldest son alone. *Women* could, however, acquire the freedom by servitude, and *their* apprentices acquired the franchise. It does not appear, however, distinctly that their sons inherited, though probably this was the case. In the year 1713, the number of free persons of Richmond was *three hundred and fifty-nine*, as was proved by the election of a Mayor at that period, which was bitterly contested. In 1727, however, the burgesses lost their right of voting for Members of Parliament, which was decided by the House of Commons to vest only in the owners of certain " burgage houses." Half a century after this, also, the trade of the town was taken out of the monopoly of the burgesses. From this the admissions by servitude declined ; and so rapid was the decay, that in A. D. 1820 the number of burgesses of Richmond was only *eighty!*

In the city of Carlisle the franchise is inherited by all the sons, and acquired by servitude. The number of the burgesses is, however, not very different from what it was a century ago, notwithstanding constant and numerous admissions by servitude. It is not a rich corporation. To multiply examples would be needless, though very easy.

Various other bodies of men may be referred to as exhibiting results precisely similar to the foregoing, and amongst these may be instanced the Society of " Friends" or " Quakers," as they were at first derisively, though now familiarly called. This sect is believed to be the most opulent, in proportion to its numbers, of all the bodies of dissenters. It keeps its own poor in so admirable a manner, that a destitute, or even apparently poor Quaker is not to be seen anywhere. In the points of morality and sobriety, the Society of Friends is perhaps unequalled by any other religious body ; consequently, the members of this wealthy and exemplary sect almost universally marry, and marry early. Yet not having been aided in modern times by conversions to their body from any other divisions of Christians to any great extent, it is believed they have decreased during the last century. They do not, as far as the author's inquiries have gone, possess any means of ascertaining their exact numbers at different periods, but this is their impression ; some may deny or doubt the decrease, but none argue for any known or sensible increase of their numbers within memory. Those who marry out of the Society are indeed expelled, at least, until the stranger's partner conform to the rules of their body ; but the loss from such expulsions, and from expulsions for other reasons, is quite insufficient to account for the non-increase of the sect. Free from intemperance of any sort, they afford one of the most striking proofs of the truth of the rule, that with generous and solid living superfluity of numbers is not to be dreaded.

Similar results are observed to occur with the Slave Population of the North American United States. It is there observed that the slaves increase, whilst the emancipated negroes decrease and gradually decay. The first are hard-worked and only moderately fed ; the second, destitute of taste for the most common luxuries, or even comforts of European or civilised life, are enabled, by a little labour, to indulge to the uttermost in the most vulgar sensualities of our nature, and hence the decay of this class which the American writers describe.

Having so far elucidated the law of decrease in such bodies of men as are possessed of means to continue that mode of living which tends to produce the *plethoric state*, it will be expected that some illustrations of the opposite tendency, the law of rapid increase, which exists amongst communities ill-fed and subjected to those privations which superinduce the law of *decrease*, or *deplethoric state*, should be given.

This is a much less easy task. Bodies of men enjoying ample means are necessarily not very extensive, and are, in a manner, insulated and marked out in society. The poor are scattered over the community, and to their circumstances, and to the effects of these circumstances on their fecundity, general references are much more easy than particular instances. Such references have already been given. The Scottish Highlands, and all Ireland, afford striking proofs of this truth. The numbers of children in maritime villages, where fish is the principal food, have been adverted to by political economists, and attempted to be explained upon their principles— the cheapness and plenty of fish being set down for the causes. No people, however, are poorer than the inhabitants of fishing villages, and it would be easy to prove that they have by no means a constant plenty even of the edible in which they deal. It is poverty, and not plenty, that stimulates their growth. The surprise of travellers, who have been accustomed to thinly-peopled countries, such as Russia and most of her tributary pastoral kingdoms, at the swarms of children in all the *poorer parts* of our cities

and towns, is another striking proof of this.
Dr. Hamel, who travelled over England at the
expense of the Russian Government, but who
was, however, a German by birth, strongly ex-
pressed his astonishment at the difference, for
which he could not account. The history of the
world, however, is not without insulated instances
of the truth of this law of increase. The most
extraordinary and striking on record is, perhaps,
to be found in the History of the Mutineer
Colony, on the desolate island of Pitcairn, in the
Pacific Ocean, about fifty years ago. This
singular colony arose out of the mutiny against
Captain Bligh, the commander of the Bounty,
on what was called the Bread Fruit Tree expedition. The ringleader of the mutineers, Fletcher
Christian, seems to have settled upon Pitcairn's
Island, after leaving most of his companions at
the Island of Otaheite, about the year 1790.
The first account of the existence of the colony
is afforded by Lieutenant Shillibeer, of the Briton,
who was there about the year 1814. Christian
seems to have landed on the island with nine
Europeans, six men of Otaheite, and eleven
Otaheitan women. One of the women, Christian's wife, died soon after their arrival, and
Christian having appropriated to himself the wife

of one of the Otaheitans, was shot by him in re-
venge, together with two other Englishmen.
This led to the murder of all the Otaheitan
males, so that the colony was at once reduced to
sixteen adult persons in all, that is to say, six
male Europeans and ten Otaheitan females.
This number was afterwards lessened to fifteen
adults by the fall of one of the men from a cliff.
When visited by Shillibeer, they had increased
their numbers to forty-eight, and this was at
most only twenty-four years after their reaching
the island.   During this period, then, they had
tripled their population, and subsequent accounts
seem to confirm the fact of this rapid increase
having continued, it having been ascertained
recently that the numbers upon the island had
reached the extraordinary height of one hundred
and eighty persons.   Adams, one of the mutineers, was still living, at the age of eighty.
Thus, in about forty years, or a little more, this
extraordinary colony seems to have decupled its
population—a rapidity of increase probably hardly
paralleled in the annals of the world.   Let us
now inquire into their mode of living, and in
that mode will be found the true solution of this
extraordinary fecundity.   The Island of Pitcairn,
when they landed upon it, seems to have been

almost devoid of the means of sustaining life, being destitute of trees bearing edible fruit, and of succulent vegetables. "The Bread Fruit and Cocoa-nut trees (says Lieutenant Shillibeer,) were brought with them in the Bounty, and have since been reared with great success." Their agriculture he describes as being confined to the *cultivation of the yam*, which they had brought to *extraordinary perfection*. Of grain they were altogether destitute. They had some poultry, and the few goats and pigs on the island were neglected, and running wild in the woods. Beyond the cultivation of the yam, the principal business of these colonists is the pursuit of *fish*, with which the coast abounds. It is, however, every way bounded with rocks, so that they are at all times obliged to carry their little boats to the village. Their light clothing was made from the bark of a tree. Here, then, we have a bird's-eye view of a mode of living singularly adapted to fecundity forced upon a limited population, and its effects. Until their fruit trees grew, which would not be for some years, fish, yams, and the eggs of their few poultry, and of wild birds, must have been their sole subsistence. This probably, together with the heat of the climate, was the foundation of the taste for the species of diet which has prevailed. There were, it is stated, a few wild rabbits on the island, but they had *not domesticated any*.

Thus, then, these islanders afford a proof at how fearful a rate population will increase amongst a people obtaining their food only by constant exertion, that food being nearly altogether fish and vegetables, and the people being destitute entirely of grain of any sort, and also of the grape, and consequently ignorant of the pernicious habit of indulging excessively in the use of fermented or distilled liquors. To account for the growth of this colony in any other way, seems to the author to be out of the question. To attribute it to *abundant food* seems perfectly absurd; for this is to assert that these poor people, whose only subsistence must frequently have been the yam, and whose only drink is water, or the milk of the cocoa-nut, lived more luxuriously, or better, not only than the free burgesses of New-castle, but also than the nobility of Venice and England! or the magnates of Geneva! To find anything resembling it, we must resort to communities living in a manner somewhat similar. On the coasts of Ireland, and amongst the Highlanders of Scotland, there can be no doubt that particular spots might be found where the increase of the people, and the number of children compared to the adults, would show a very high ratio. A part of the result at Pitcairn's Island, however, must be doubtless attributed to the remote situation and great salubrity of the climate and of the place, which seems to have given to the inhabitants an immunity from those infectious and epidemic diseases to which the poor of other countries are so peculiarly and fatally liable. It must also be remembered that the colonists of Pitcairn's Island were never actually thinned by *direct famine*, as the thickly peopled countries always are ; a truth to which the annals of China, Hindostan, Ireland, and the Scotch Islands bear horrible testimony. Another less well-authenticated instance of increase, under somewhat similar circumstances, is to be found in the historical tradition of the Catheran, Sawney, or Donald Bane or Bean. This man is recorded to have lived about the year 1600, in the reign of James the Sixth, of Scotland (our James the First), on the coast of Galloway. Immured, for the sake of concealment, in an immense cavern, this man is supposed to have carried on the trade of freebooter for a series of twenty-five years ; and (if the legends as to his life are to be believed) to have lived, in some part, upon the flesh of his murdered victims. That he and his family should, at times, have been driven by famine to such a resource is not incredible; but that he should have preferred this mode of sustenance is clearly a feature of the story which the atrocity of the entire circumstances would recommend to popular credulity. The facts seem to be, that, after living this sort of life for a full quarter of a century, this wretch and his family were captured and put to death at Edinburgh; when, it should seem, that the incestuous progeny of the atrocious couple were eight sons and six daughters, who again had produced eighteen grandsons and fourteen grand-daughters, the whole family being *forty-eight*, or twenty-seven males and twenty-one females! The data of their numbers, and their general mode of life, are probably quite correct. The results are the same as those of the colony at Pitcairn's Island; but it is difficult to believe that in *twenty-five years* one couple could have been the origin of such a multitude. The probability is, that a somewhat longer time than twenty-five years had elapsed before their capture. The result, however, is extraordinary.

With these examples the author must conclude this chapter. It would not be difficult to add to the number of such exemplifications. Enough, however, has probably been done to prove, to the satisfaction of the reader, the clear existence of the law of increase and of decrease amongst limited bodies of men, when under certain circumstances. It seems evident that where men are living in a state of ease and plenty, their tendency certainly is *not* to keep up their numbers, but the contrary. Thus we see that the nobility and very wealthy and highly privileged classes of all nations are in a continual state of decay; that such have been the facts with the English nobility and the English baronets—that such has been the case with the Venetian nobility; and again, that such was the case with the ancient Roman nobility. Going a little lower, we see the same rapid decay amongst the rich Swiss bourgeoisie, who are a sort of nobility. Going a little lower than that, we find the same tendency to a failure of the line amongst the wealthy free burgesses of the English boroughs. This, however, is in a mitigated degree; and in the less wealthy boroughs, we perceive the decreasing tendency lessening, and almost at a stay.

Turning to the other side of the question, and contemplating the few examples attainable of limited bodies of men subjected to privation, we see the tendency to rapid increase most strikingly developed. In Pitcairn's Island we discover, amongst the colony of Adams and his mutineer companions, proofs of a stride in population far exceeding the most extravagant ideas of the most extravagant advocates for a reduplicating geometrical ratio. But then we find this accompanied with the absence of solid food, and with constant toil and exposure to the open air, and the vicissitudes of the climate. In the strange story of Donald Bean, the same results are developed, living amidst all the vicissitudes of an outlaw, often in total want of food, and probably never well supplied, the increase of these wretched beings seems to have been extraordinary, and certainly to be accounted for in the same manner as that of Adams' colony.

It will be the business of the next chapter to apply the same method of inquiry to larger bodies of men ; to try to evolve the same results from the statistics of nations ; and to demonstrate that, if put into a certain state, a whole people may exhibit the same results as a more limited body exhibits, and that depletion and low diet, whether amongst nations or families, is followed by an overabundant fecundity; whilst, on the other hand, luxury, solid living, and repletion, are the sure drag and stay to the onward progress of population.

CHAPTER V.

THE LAW OF INCREASE AND DECREASE, AS EXEMPLIFIED AMONGST NATIONS.

THE author would now draw attention to the statistical facts as to such nations of the globe as are at all accurately known, with the view of inquiring how these facts bear out the foregoing theory—they will, he believes, be found to do so with wonderful accuracy. It will be found, on examination, that such countries as are over-peopled are exclusively agricultural, and dependent upon vegetable food. That, on the contrary, the pastoral countries, where animal food and milk are the support of the people, their numbers are always low. In countries where the two modes prevail the population is a medium as to number between the two extremes. The cultivation of the vine and olive, and the use of their rich products as ordinary articles of diet, will also always be found to be connected with a somewhat moderate population. Such are the general results which are to be deduced from the following details to which the author now proceeds.

The statistics of the Russian empire, including as it does various races of people living in climates the most different, upon soils the most opposite in quality, and all under one government, foreign to each other as they are in habits, customs, modes of life and language, afford perhaps the most striking and curious exemplification of the effects upon population caused by different modes of living. The immense area of the Russian empire—that is to say, all its Asiatic, and a large portion of its European dominions—is inhabited by a people the most truly pastoral of any existing in the world. Their wealth is cattle. Their exports are the tallow, hides, and horns. Their food is the flesh. Agriculture, as a means of subsistence, is of no value. Their summer is brief and sudden—it grazes and it fodders their herds of cattle, but beyond this is nothing. Vegetable aliment is a mere fraction in the food of the population—and what bread is in countries less pastoral, beef is to the Russian boor and his scarcely more cultivated master. It is impossible that the fact should have been otherwise. Where the cattle are slaughtered for the sake of the tallow and hides, the flesh must, as a matter of course, be the food of the people. It is so plentiful as to be almost valueless. In the capital of St. Petersburgh even, excellent beef is always to be had at about the price of an English penny per lb. Three halfpence per lb. is a rare price to anybody, and under any circumstances; and yet the herds of cattle which supply the capital are driven from very great distances. Throughout not only the capital towns, but the whole empire, frozen game of all descriptions is plentiful in the extreme; and the rich and oily flesh of the salmon and the sturgeon, pickled or salted, form an ingredient of this rich dietary from which also the less delicate oil of the whale and seal are by no means excluded, though not prominently brought forward. The kingdom of Poland, however, and the Russian provinces bordering on Russian Poland, are essentially corn countries, and hence the food of their people is totally and altogether different. Wheat, rye, and barley are the staple commodities of these countries: they are consequently the principal aliment of the inhabitants. Thus the food of the people of Russian Poland, Courland, &c., is the exact opposite of that of the other inhabitants of the immense territories of the Czars; and from these opposite States, effects the most opposite have been produced. The consequence has been, that the population of the corn countries, compared with the rest, has been as five to one! Nor have political circumstances in the slightest degree interfered to bring about these results, but the contrary. The serfs being the most valuable part of the stock of an estate, the Russian landlord, so far from wishing to clear his lands, counts up his boors as he does his cattle, by the head, wishing both to increase and multiply; and it is well known to all who know Russia, that the conscriptions for the army are felt to be more grievous when directed towards the two-legged, rather than the four-legged inhabitants of the lordship. Bearing, then, all these circumstances in mind, let us look at the broad facts, as stated in " M. Hassel's Tables of the Population of Russia," as represented by Malte Brun. These tables are beyond a doubt substantially correct. They were compiled and published under the sanction and supervision of the Russian Government, and if error there be, the side of paucity of numbers is not that on which the error was likely to be made. In using these tables, it must be premised that the *Russian square mile* of M. Hassel is equal to *twenty* English square miles, or rather more than *two English square leagues.*

RUSSIA.

Grand Divisions.	Square miles in it.	Population.	Number to a square mile.
RUSSIAN EMPIRE . . (divided into)	367,494	59,263,700	161
European Asia	72,861	44,118,600	606
Kingdom of Poland . .	2,293	3,541,900	1,544
Asiatic Russia	268,339	11,663,200	43⅛
American Russia . . .	24,000	50,000	2¼

Here, then, taking the grand divisions alone into view, it results that, in the kingdom of Poland, where corn rather than animal food is the aliment of the people, but at the same time with an abundance of it, the numbers upon a Russian square mile are, upon the average, 1,544 individuals, or nearly *ten times* the average to the square mile, including the whole empire. If more minute divisions are taken, similar results are exhibited. In the Duchy of Courland and in Western Russia, for instance, the results are as follow : —These countries border upon Poland, and are similarly circumstanced, being essentially corn countries. In order to show that this population is spread equally over

the surface of these countries, and not caused
by masses of people collected by local circumstances into large towns, the population of each
government, as stated in the Russian statistical
tables, is given. Thus, there is no room for
doubt as to the population being the natural
population of these countries.

Division.	Square miles in each.	Population.	Persons to a square mile.
COURLAND	509	581,300	1,142
WESTERN RUSSIA . . .	7,537	8,488,900	1,125
(including)			
Government of Wilna . .	1,081	1,357,400	1,255
. . Grodno .	326	868,100	1,619
. . Bivlystock	158	224,600	1,422
. . Witepsk .	668	934,900	1,398
. . Mohileu .	918	985,400	1,073
. . Minsk . .	1,832	1,160,100	633
. . Volhynia .	1,394	1,496,300	1,072
. . Podolia .	948	1,462,190	1,542

Such are the results of a comparison of the
population calculated upon the square Russian
mile, as afforded by the corn-growing countries
of the Russian empire. With the single exception of the government of Minsk, the peopling
of each district is somewhere between (1,000)
one thousand and (1,600) sixteen hundred to the
Russian square mile. If these districts be so
compared to the most fertile, pastoral, or cattle-

feeding districts of the Muscovite dominion, the result will be found to be very striking. In short, it will be found that the regions most fertile in cattle, or, in other words, *animal food*, are the least so in men.

Let us take, for example, the kingdoms of Astrakhan and of Kasan. They are amongst the finest pastoral provinces of Russia, and from the last (Kasan) comes a considerable portion of the tallow exported by the Russians. It is of fine quality throughout, though perhaps less skilfully dealt with than the tallow from the Southern provinces of the empire, properly so called. This is a proof, as far as it goes, that the cattle are not only completely, but slowly fattened, and that no exigencies of the population render it necessary to bring them prematurely to market, or to slaughter them when in imperfect condition. Astrakhan is less rich.

Names of divisions.	Square miles in each.	Population.	People to each mile.
KINGDOM OF KASAN . (including)	11,521	5,746,250	498
Government of Kasan . .	1,123	1,028,150	915
. . Viatka. .	2,221	1,293,800	582
. . Perm . .	5,996	1,269,900	212
. . Simbrisk .	1,402	1,119,400	798
. . Pensa . .	777	1,035,000	1,331

Names of divisions.	Square miles in each.	Population.	People to each mile.
KINGDOM OF ASTRAKHAN (including)	13,823	2,598,700	118
Government of Astrakhan	3,899	222,700	57
. . Sawtow .	4,297	1,333,500	310
. . Orenburgh	5,626	1,043,500	185

Such are the states of populousness of the districts or kingdoms of Kasan and Astrakhan—two countries both fertile and pastoral in a great degree.

The most decidedly pastoral districts of the Russian empire are, however, those comprised in the fine region emphatically called Southern Russia.

Upon these immense and beautiful plains, or undulating tracts, are the countless herds of cattle reared and fed from which is derived the greater portion of the tallow and skins which form the grand articles of export from the Russian empire. From these distant grazing lands a constant driving of herds of cattle goes on, and the expense of this driving fixes principally the value and price of the tallow. Hence, at high prices, it has been found that there is hardly a limit to the possible supply. The cattle are driven so slowly as to be fattened, and kept fat, as they move on towards the place of slaughter, and some of the nobles over whose estates they pass, derive large revenues from this source alone. Some years ago Count Orloff received annually 30,000 roubles in tolls of this sort from a single estate—being upon 120,000 head of cattle at the rate of 25 copeaks per head. The ultimate destination of these herds is the town of Columna, or Kolumna, which is one immense slaughter-shop, the greatest in all Russia. Thence the tallow is brought to the coast for shipment. Let us now look at the population of Southern Russia, and also at the Slobodes of the Ukraine, which also help to produce these countless herds. It is as follows :—

Name of District.	Square Russian miles.	Population.	Numbers to a mile.
SOUTHERN RUSSIA, . . (including)	8772	2,316,600	265
Government of Ichatuinoslaw.	1417	826,100	583
. . Kersou .	1206	459,400	380
. . Taurida .	1646	346,200	211
. . Don Cossacks	3611	369,800	102
SLOBODES OF UKRAINE .	1118	914,400	817

Thus, in the most pastoral provinces, where the cattle are the sole produce, and the sole food almost of the people, the numbers are lowest. In short, in Southern Russia, the pastoral district, the population to the square mile is not one-sixth that of the corn country, Poland.

With this state of population as existing throughout these immense pastoral districts, let us contrast the state of countries equally extensive, but pursuing a mode of life precisely opposite to that of the Russian serfs.

The countries of China, Japan, and Hindostan present perhaps the most striking example of the the effects of a diet, nearly altogether vegetable, upon a people. In the first of these countries the people seem to have spontaneously for ages given the preference to agriculture, and neglected the rearing of animal food, until the density of the population has rendered it no longer practicable if a change were contemplated. In Japan the government itself interferes, and compels its people to cultivate vegetable rather than rear animal food. In Hindostan, the Brahminical religion interferes to prevent the shedding of the blood of animals. Hence in China, horned cattle and sheep are almost unknown, and in Japan totally so. In British India flesh-meat is only eaten by the European and Mahometan part of

the population. If we look at the statistical
details of these countries, we shall find a redun-
dancy of population to an enormous extent.
With regard to the two first mentioned, we are
certainly without those minute and highly accurate details which we possess as to Russia and
some other countries. But enough is known to
shew the certainty that such is the truth; and
the accounts of the population of British India
fully bear out the more general statements as to
the numbers inhabiting the two first mentioned.

The area of China Proper, is in round numbers one million two hundred and ninety-eight
thousand square miles, or one hundred and forty-
five square leagues—as to its precise population there is certainly some dispute. It was
estimated by Father Allerstein in 1743, and again
by Lord Macartney in 1795, upon the testimony
of the Chinese authorities. Both of these estimates were sanctioned by men who had intimate
or personal knowledge of the country in question;
both, however, have been disputed. Let us first
take the estimates themselves, and then examine
the grounds of objection : –

POPULATION OF CHINA.

Provinces.	Allerstein, 1743.	Macartney, 1795.
Fongtain	668,852	} 38,000,000
Petchili	15,222,940	
Kiangnan	45,922,439	32,000,000
Kiangsi	11,006,604	19,000,000
Tchekiang.	15,429,690	21,000,000
Foukien	8,063,671	15,000,000
Hooquang.	16,910,423	27,000,000
Shanton	25,180,734	24,000,000
Honan	16,332,507	25,000,000
Chansi	9,768,189	27,000,000
Chinese division Singan	7,287,443	18,000,000
—————— Kansoo	7,412,014	12,000,000
Sc-tchooen	2,782,976	27,000,000
Koo-ang-Tong . . .	6,782,975	21,000,000
Koo-ang-Si	3,947,414	10,000,000
Yoonan	2,078,892	8,000,000
Koeicheoo	3,402,722	9,000,000
Total	198,213,713	333,000,000

These estimates are objected to by M. Malte Brun, who seems eager to depreciate the Chinese as a nation. He is one of those writers who seem to be thoroughly possessed with the notion that population is one of the tests of prosperity and industry, and he accordingly taxes his ingenuity to bring together objections to the probability of the accounts of the dense population of these regions. His objections are, first, that there are something like repetitions of the

names of the provinces, as given by Macartney
and Allerstein : secondly, that the disproportion
between the two as to numbers is incredible :
lastly, that in the time of the Emperor Kienlong,
the peasants liable to tribute were only twenty-
five millions. It is curious enough that in the
table giving the proportion of tax paid by each
province, the same names exactly are given as
those in Macartney and Allerstein's population
tables. The result is as follows :—

Number of Peasants subject to the Tribute.	Tribute in Wheat in Chinese bushels.	Tribute of Silver in hand.
25,165,390	6,396,286	28,360,800
	Bushel, 12,070 Cubic Inches, French.	Lana, 709 Dutch *As*.

He also gives the ancient statements as
to population, which are certainly far below
the modern statements. It is to be doubted,
however, if these statements included the whole
of what is mapped as modern China Proper.
The ancient statements are as follow, and they
exhibit, if at all accurate, some remarkable fluctuations in the *rates of fecundity*.

	Families.	Mouths.
Census in the First Century .	12,233,062	59,594,978
A.D. 740, Tang Dynasty . .	8,412,800	48,143,600
A.D. 1393, Hong Voo . . .	16.052,860	60,545,812
A.D. 1491, Hiao Tsoug. . .	9,113,446	53,281,158
A.D. 1578, Van Lie	10,621,436	60,692,856

The author gives the above, not as bearing much upon the question of the present numbers of the Chinese nation, but as exhibiting remarkable fluctuations of population, resulting altogether from a change of fecundity amongst the same people. The first census, on comparison of the mouths to the families, gives not quite *five* to each family. In the year 740 the fecundity has increased to *six* the average family ; in 1393 the population has doubled, but from some cause a decrease takes place in the rate of fecundity, and the average family is under *four* ; in 1491 the people are again decreased nearly a half, but the average family is nearly *six* persons ; in 1578 the average family is *six*, and population increasing. To what these changes of fecundity are owing, it would now be difficult to trace ; but of the changes having taken place, there seems to be fair evidence.

Let us return, however, to the objections of
M. Malte Brun. It seems clear enough that no
faith in the accuracy of Lord Macartney's account can be entertained, the Mandarins having
palpably arranged the numbers so as to give
333,000,000. But it does not at all follow that
the truth does not lie between this account and
that of Father Allerstein in 1743. So far is the
result of the tribute table from *weakening
Allerstein's account*, that it confirms it. It is
well known that if those capable of bearing arms
in a country be selected, they will be found to
amount only to about a sixth part of the people,
but the persons or peasants liable to pay this tax
were clearly only a portion of the adult male
population. If any females were liable they must
have been few in number, there being few unmar-
ried females in China ; and of the adult males, all
the privileged orders, all the very poor, all the
soldiery, all the seamen, all the other employes
of government, and all those who in any way
evaded the tribute, must probably be deducted.
If then, as is not unlikely, the persons subject
to, and paying this tribute, confined as it was to
wheat and silver, were not more than a *seventh*
or *eighth* part of the entire community, Allerstein's account is confirmed by the result. From

1743, the date of Allerstein's calculation, to 1795, that of Lord Macartney's, is a period of half a century. What improbability is there then, in the supposition that during this period the population of this densely peopled region, as it is known to be, may not have reached 250,000,000 or 280,000,000 of persons ? Taking the area at 145,000 square leagues, this would give 1724 persons in the first case, and 1931 in the second case, to each league; a result the reverse of improbable, when Ireland and some of the poorer European countries are looked at, where the food of the inhabitants is vegetable for the most part, as in China. Throughout the whole of the Celestial Empire this is certainly the fact. Rice is the principal aliment, and tea or water the beverage of the people. There are no fermented liquors, and fewer animals of any sort than in any other country, the Japanese Islands perhaps excepted. On the coasts fish is abundant, as well as in the great rivers, upon which last two millions of people are believed to pass their lives in crafts of various kinds. The whole interior is known to be in a high state of cultivation, and early and universal marriages are enjoined by the State. The density of the population is admitted by all travellers; and it has

long been known that in China, everything that
that admits of it is made available for food, and
that rats and other vermin are eagerly eaten
by the natives. If to this is added the mortality
and exposure of children, which since Lord
Macartney's embassy is undoubted, we have
every reason to believe that his general view of
the immense extent of Chinese population accords
with truth, though the folly of the Mandarins
has thrown discredit upon their statements.
Under any view, if China, where there is no
animal food, be contrasted with Russia, where
there is little else, it is impossible not to be
struck with the difference of the two countries in
this particular, similar as they are in some other
essential points. In the Empire of Japan we
find similar causes producing similar effects. In
these Islands agriculture, to the total exclusion
of pasturage, is enjoined by law, and the consequence is a total want of animal food, as well as
of the animals which might afford it. Thunberg
states, that in his time there were probably more
horses in a province of Sweden than in all the
Japanese Empire. Of the larger cattle there are
none, and goats and sheep are totally banished.
Cotton and silk supply the place of wool. There
are a few swine in the vicinity of Nangasacki,
and superstition has saved the lives of a few

dogs. Since the expulsion of the missionaries in 1630, the jealousy of the Japanese has excluded the country almost from the knowledge of Europeans. It is quite certain, however, that the aliment of the people is vegetable, and the population is dense in the extreme for a country so mountainous and the reverse of fertile. Golownin, a Russian naval officer, who with his crew was imprisoned there in 1811, 1812, and 1813, bears general testimony to the immense population of such places as he saw during his detention; his evidence as to diet is also decisive. The food he partook of was generally rice cooked in different ways, soup composed generally of radishes with wild herbs and seasonings, salted or fresh fish, and fruit. The beverage was water, tea, or a small beer, made by fermenting rice called sagi. He describes the Japanese as accounting not only all sorts of fish, but all marine vegetables, as eatable. The fish on the coasts seem to be very plentiful, and the modes of taking them wonderfully successful. His detention lasted upwards of two years; during that time he tasted of three or four fowls, eggs occasionally, and as a treat on his release, of ducks, geese, and game; but of anything like butcher's meat there was a total absence. The Dutch writers confirm these accounts. They describe the soil as sterile, but cultivated with prodigious care even high up the mountains. All accounts concur in describing the population of the habitable parts as dense in the extreme. The capital city, Jeddo, is believed to be the largest in the world, and to contain 1,680,000 inhabitants. The armies maintained by the Keebo, or military dictator, and the federal tributary Princes, are said to amount to 468,000 infantry and 53,000 cavalry, for which purpose alone horses are bred by the government. They have little or no marine, and now are nearly without foreign trade. The most striking proof, however, of the " prodigious population " of these islands, is to be found in the amount of the revenue. This is stated by Varencies, a well-informed Dutch author, at the enormous sum of *two thousand eight hundred and thirty-four* Dutch tons of gold, which, valuing the ton at ten thousand pounds, will be upwards of *twenty millions sterling.* And this (says M. Malte Brun) is without reckoning the provinces and towns which depend immediately on the Emperor.

It is impossible to conceive that sums so enormous should be levied directly from a people destitute of foreign commerce, and inhabiting a country not exuberantly rich, unless that people were very numerous. The area of the empire is estimated to be 266,500 square miles English, or 29,600 square leagues. Malte Brun, who admits its "prodigious" density, (as is usual with him in speaking of these regions) under-rates the amount of population, which he calls thirty millions. It is believed, however, to be about forty-five millions, which gives in round numbers 1,500 persons to the square league; a wonderful proportion, when it is considered that these islands consist mostly of mountains; that the soil is comparatively sterile, as compared with continental Asia, and the climate inclement, the highest peaks being covered with snow all the year.

Many readers will, perhaps, hesitate as to what reliance should be placed upon the foregoing statements, relating as they do to regions as to which our statistical knowledge is confessedly very defective, and only general. Nor would such hesitation be improper, were it not luckily the case that ample and complete corroboration is at hand in the statistics of regions very similar in the habits of their inhabitants, and as to which our knowledge is perfect and undoubted. The regions in question are the British territories in India, and those of the allies and tributaries of the British Government, together with the few independent States, forming altogether the immense territory of

Hindostan. Of the larger portion of the natives
of these regions, it is notorious that their religion, which is Brahminical, forbids the use of
animal food. The heat of the climate conspires
with their superstition to prohibit the resort to
animal food. It is accordingly hardly eaten
at all, excepting by the European residents,
the richer Mahometans, and a few of the degra-
ded native castes, who, however, cannot obtain
much from the want of means. Rice, of which
there are *twenty-seven* Indian varieties, is the
principal food, in point of fact, of *all* classes,
Europeans hardly excepted. Upon it the
native inhabitants depend for subsistence; and
a failure in the rice crop occasions a famine,
to which, for extent of suffering, no dearth in
European countries can be compared. These
famines are not unfrequent, and are thought,
at times, to have caused the death of hundreds
of thousands of persons. The different tribes
are often in a state of warfare. The Asiatic
Cholera, never wholly extinguished, from time
to time, destroys its millions, yet all these causes
of diminution have not sufficed to keep down
the population of these regions, which, in the
level and cultivated parts, is wonderfully dense.
Of British India, indeed of Hindostan, the
finest portion is unquestionably the province

of Bengal. It is situated on the lower part of the course of the great river Ganges, which divides into two parts nearly equal. It is fertile in the extreme, and highly cultivated. The climate, however, is very unhealthy, an insalubrity which is increased by the mode of cultivating rice, which is irrigated from large standing pools of water, artificially embanked by the cultivator. Southern Bengal produces no other edible grain; but as the country rises towards the north, wheat, barley, and the potato are also grown. The rivers, as well as the coasts, abound in fish. Such is the food of Bengal, and the following table will show its effects on the population; of its general accuracy there can be no doubt :—

POPULATION OF THE BENGAL PRESIDENCY FOR 1820.

Territories.	British square mile.	Population.	Numbers to the square league.
Bengal, Bahar, and Benares	162,000	39,000,000	2,166
Additions since 1765 . .	148,000	18,000,000	1,094
Gurwal Kumaoon, and tracts between Sulledge and Jumna }	18,000	500,000	250

Thus we see that in the old and completely cultivated territory of Bengal, where rice and fish are the food of the natives, the population has reached the enormous amount of *two thou-*

sand one hundred and sixty-six persons to each British square league, a strong corroboration of the truth of the alleged populousness of China, which has been for time immemorial under a similarly high state of cultivation.

The two other Presidencies of Madras and Bombay are not only much more mountainous, and far less fertile, but are also far less completely cleared and cultivated. The territories of the British tributaries, and those of the allies and the independent States, are similarly circumstanced. Much of their surface is yet forest, mountain, swamp, and jungle, the habitation of the elephant and the tiger, the buffalo and the rhinoceros : yet even here the population to the square league British is not less, or much less, than *one thousand* on the average, an extraordinary one for a tract where cultivation is almost confined to the banks of the rivers. The following will shew the result : —

Territory.	British square miles.	Population.	Numbers to the square league.
Madras Presidency . .	154,000	15,000,000	882
Bombay Presidency . .	11,000	2,500,000	2,049
Deccan	60,000	8,000,000	1,201
Total	225,000	25,500,000	1,020

The next table shews the population of some
of the territories of the principal tributaries and
allies of the British :—

Territory.	British square miles.	Population.	Number to the square league.
The Nizam	96,000	10,000,000	1,000 nearly.
The Nagpoon Raja . .	70,000	3,000,000	390
The King of Oude . .	20,000	3,000,000	1,363
The Guicowas . . .	18,000	2,000,000	1,000
The Mysore Raja . .	27,000	3,000,000	1,000
The Satanah Raja . .	14,000	1,500,000	937
Travancou and Cochen	8,000	1,000,000	1,100
Kotah Brondu Bossaul	14,000	1,500,000	937

Of the independent States, which are only five,
the dominions of Scindia and Afghan territory are
the most fertile and populous, and they give similar results.   Nepaul is the poorest, most rocky,
and least populous. Such is the population of those
portions of Asia, where climate, soil, religion, and
manners have united to force a diet of vegetables
only upon the inhabitants.   If we turn to Europe,
and examine those countries where poverty or
any other cause has induced similar modes of
living, we shall find the results to be similar.
This populousness then does not arise from
climate, or any peculiar physical constitution of
the people, but from the nature of their food,

and its restricted quantity.; in short, from poverty
of diet in quality or in quantity, or in both.

Ireland is beyond a question the poorest
country, as to the destitute state of its population, of all Europe, perhaps of the whole globe.
Of a population of *eight millions of persons,* it
has been ascertained after an inquiry instituted
by Parliament, that not less than *two millions
and a quarter* are wandering and houseless
mendicants, subsisting upon the charity of their
hardly richer brethren. The owners of the land
to a great extent spend their incomes in other
countries. There is no efficient Poor-law to
oppose a check to destitution and starvation.
The dignitaries of the Establishment do not
reside on their benefices, and spend their tithes
in many instances in England altogether, or on
the continent ; whilst the Roman Catholic
church is too poor to allow its ministers to
alleviate by charity the sufferings of the people.
In this state of poverty the mode of living of a
people so destitute may be easily conjectured.
Dwelling for the most part in mud cabins, without
window or chimney, save a hole in the wall or
roof, and shivering over a fire of peat, they live
almost solely on the potatoes which they raise
upon their little holdings ; their children par-

taking, perhaps, of the milk of their cow, if they possess one. Of clothing proper for the climate they are as destitute as they are of proper aliment, and the pig of the Irish peasant is often as well fed, and little less profusely bedded and clothed, than himself. In point of fact, not only all the live stock of every description, but every edible, whether in the shape of cured provisions, wheat, barley, peas, beans, butter or lard, is exported from Ireland and consumed, the only exception being the potato. The cottager who tastes bacon four times a year is a lucky man, and a little whisky forms his sole departure from the beverage of nature, water. The money amount of Irish cattle and provisions of all sorts *imported into the town of Liverpool alone* in the year 1831, was estimated to be as high as £4,497,708.

In 1832, the returns give £4,444,500 as the value.

Nor is this state of things without its drawbacks upon the increase, real or apparent, of the Irish population. The poverty of the country and the prevalence of distress, cause a constant emigration of all who can find the means to leave it. Every year numbers ship themselves for the United States, or for the British settlements in

America. Greater numbers still cross the Irish Sea to the West of England and Scotland, and making their way to the Metropolis and to the great towns, continue there as labourers. Numbers enter the army, and many the navy. In Ireland itself, constantly recurring scarcities of the potato crop, attended with the malignant fevers which ever accompany dearth, thin for a time whole districts. Civil wars and oppressions have also done much to keep down the numbers of this unfortunate race. From the time of the Reformation, under Henry VIII., to the Protectorate of Cromwell, Ireland presents a scene of slaughters, rebellions, and bloodshed, under every form. Again, at the Revolution of 1688, Irish blood flowed in torrents in behalf of the exiled family. Since that period the Orange Protestant party have held the Roman Catholics under constant persecutions and oppressions; yet has this miserable population gone on rapidly increasing, and making more and more rapid head against all these numerous apparent causes of diminution and extermination.

At the close of Elizabeth's reign the Irish people remaining were estimated, probably erroneously, to be no more than *seven hundred thousand* in all!

Sir William Petty conjectures the population, at the close of the wars in 1652, to have been about *eight hundred and fifty thousand souls;* which he supposes increased to *one million one hundred thousand persons* in 1672. Subsequent investigators have arrived at the following conclusions. They are no doubt founded on different data, and only amount to probable guesses at, or approximations to the truth. They prove that in the space of one hundred and thirty years the population of Ireland has more than *quadrupled* itself, and that it has increased, as distress and poverty and want of food increased, with an accelerated velocity, as if the pressure caused by its own density urged it forward.

ESTIMATED POPULATION OF IRELAND AT VARIOUS PERIODS.

				Persons.
1695	by	Captain South, at	. . .	1,034,102
1712	.	Thomas Dobbs, Esq.	. .	2,099,094
1718	.	The same	. . .	2,169,048
1726	.	The same	. . .	2,309,106
1731	.	The Established Clergy	.	2,010,221
1754	.	Hearth Money Collectors	.	2,372,634
1767	.	The same	. . .	2,544,276
1777	.	The same	. . .	2,690,556
1785	.	The same	. . .	2,845,932
1788	.	Gerv. Parker Bushe, Esq.	. .	4,040,000
1791	.	Hearth Money Collectors	.	4,206,612
1792	.	Rev. Aug. Beaufort	.	4,088,226
1805	.	Thomas Newnham, Esq.	.	5,395,456
1813	.	Incomplete Parliamentary Census	.	5,937,856
1821	.	Parliamentary Census	.	6,801,827
1831	.	Parliamentary Census	.	7,734,365

Of the whole number thus ascertained by the census of 1821, which was the most carefully taken, it was found that 1,138,069 were employed in agriculture; 1,170,044 in various trades, handicrafts, and manufactures; and that 528,702 were employed in other avocations, not included in the foregoing, making the total of employed persons 2,836,815 only. If the rate on increase, as indicated by these returns be taken, the present population of Ireland cannot be calculated at less than *eight millions and a half*. Let us now see the proportion of people to the *square British league* upon the total area of the country. Ireland is held to consist, by one estimate as ordered by Parliament, of 19,441,944 statute acres, and by another of 20,399,608 statute acres. Its area in square British miles has been calculated at 31,875 square miles; and by Wakefield and Arrowsmith, at 32,201 square miles. *Thirty-two thousand*, in round numbers, is probably near the truth. Reducing this to square leagues, and dividing the population by their number, the result is as nearly as possible, *two thousand three hundred and ninety-one persons to the square British league;* a population rivalling those of India and China---the uncultivated land, bog, and

lake being to the cultivated land as follows, in
round numbers about *six to fourteen*.

Cultivated.	Mountain and Bog.	Lakes.	Total in Statute Acres.
14,603,473	5,340,736	455,399	20,399,608

When to this we add the fact, that the cultivation of Ireland, owing to the poverty and ignorance
of the inhabitants, is miserably defective, this
result is certainly extraordinary.

We now turn to England herself; and England,
perhaps, of all countries of this globe, exhibits
phenomena the most puzzling to an inquiry of
the nature of that which forms the subject of
this treatise. Manifesting as she does all the
signs of external wealth and power, these mani-
festations are yet accompanied by symptoms
indicating a situation the reverse of prosperity;
an increasing and alarming poor's-rate, a growth
of crime, and a too rapidly augmenting population. The question, then, to be solved is this;
does this increasing population, linked as it is
with an increase of poor, with augmented poor-
rates, and augmented crime, and with other

evidence of a deteriorating condition of the labouring classes, prove, in spite of the contrary indications of wealth amongst other classes, the probable truth of the theory which forms the subject of this essay? In the author's opinion it certainly does prove this truth. If it does so, it must certainly, however, prove another collateral or correlative truth; that is to say, that the condition of the majority of the English people has, for a series of years, been *deteriorating* and still *continues to deteriorate.* That this is *a consequence,* according to the theory of population here propounded, the author willingly admits, believing it, as he does, to be indubitably true *in point of fact.* The proofs of this truth appear to him to be apparent in the following statistical facts:—1. The increased poor's-rate: 2. The increase of crime: 3. The diminished consumption of malt. In his general remarks upon these points he will not, in this division of his work, go far back; he will contrast the sum levied for the poor in 1670 with those levied since that time; but, upon the other points in question, he will merely avail himself of the evidence of the modern time, and content himself with showing that it sufficiently accounts for the increased population of this country throughout the last half or three quarters of a century. Let us first see what has been the known progress of the population of Great Britain, and then compare with its increase that of poor's-rate and crime. As for the diminished consumption of malt, that is a fact of general notoriety, and is known to be certain from the different Excise returns of the duty. The following table shows the progress of the population of England, Wales, and Scotland, separately as well as jointly : —

SUMMARY OF THE POPULATION OF GREAT BRITAIN.

	1801.	Increase per cent.	1811.	Increase per cent.	1821.	Increase per cent.	1831.
England	8,381,434	14⅔	9,551,888	17⅞	11,261,437	16	13,089,338
Wales .	541,546	14	611,788	17	717,438	12	805,236
Scotland	1, 909,068	13	2,185,688	16	2,093,456	—	2,365,807
Army & Navy }	470,598	—	640,500	—	319,300	—	277,017
Totᵣ¹	10,942,646	15¼	12,989,864	14	14,391,631	15	16,537,398

Thus the population of England has, it seems, increased between 1801 and 1831 as 9 is to 14, and that Scotland has nearly kept pace with this. The following are the returns of the amount of poor's-rate levied in the different years given. They are extracted from returns ordered by Parliament:—

Year.	Amount of Poor Rate.
1673	£ 840,000
1698	819,000
1700	1,000,000
1776	1,720,316
	Average.
1783 ⎫	
1784 ⎬	2,167,748
1785 ⎭	
1801	4,800,000 (probably).
1803	5,348,204
1812-13	8,640,842
1820-21	8,411,893
1821-22	7,761,441
1823-24	6,898,153
1830	8,111,422
1831	8,279,217

The author has been unable to ascertain the amount of rate for 1801, but it was certainly not more than five millions, although the two years preceding had been years of scarcity, amounting almost to famine. The nominal increase of the rates then from 1801 to 1831 may be stated as from 5 to 8, but the real increase is *much* greater, inasmuch as allowance for the alteration in the value of money brought about by the Currency Bill of 1819, which is generally known by the title of Mr. Peel's Bill. What the exact enhancement of the value of the currency was after 1829, when the Bill was carried into its fullest effect, the author will not here attempt to determine. It is sufficient that it is generally admitted to have been considerable; and that, upon the *lowest computation* of the value added to money by the extinction of the Bank-notes under five pounds in 1829, the poor's-rate of 1831 must have been more than double that of 1801 in reality, though not in name.

Of the increase of crime the evidence is not less decisive. In 1827 a Committee of the House of Commons appointed to inquire into this subject, not only fully admitted in their Report the fact of this alarming increase, but adduced evidence unquestionable of it. The following table of commitments is extracted from the Appendix of the Report of 1827. It is appalling.

COMMITMENTS FOR ENGLAND AND WALES FROM 1806 TO 1826 INCLUSIVE.

(Extracted from Appendix of Commons Report, 1827.

1806.	1810.	1811.	1812.	1813.	1814.
4,346	5,146	5,337	6,576	7,164	6,390

1815.	1816.	1817.	1818.	1819.	1820.
7,818	9,091	13,932	13,567	14,254	13,710

1821.	1822.	1823.	1824.	1825.	1826.
13,115	12,241	12,263	13,698	14,437	16,147

That this enormous increase—the commitments of 1826 almost quadrupling those of 1806—has been caused by distress is evident from the table itself. The first great increase is in 1817, when the revulsions in commerce caused by the end of the war produced excessive manufacturing pressure and difficulty, from which the population generally seem never to have recovered. In 1822, when, owing to the preparations for withdrawing the Country Bank paper below notes for *five pounds*, the prices of provisions were greatly lowered, an amendment in morals seems to have followed. This is again extinguished by the rise in prices and monetary crisis of 1825-6, and since that period, crime in England has gone on increasing year by year.

The following table is extracted from Official Returns on this subject up to 1834 :—

1827.	1828.	1829.	1830.
17,924	16,564	18,675	18,107

1831.	1832.	1833.	1834.
19,647	20,829	20,072	22,451

Thus the commitments of 1834 *quintuple* those of 1806 ; a growth prodigious, and only to be accounted for by the fact of an *increasing pressure* upon the lower classes of this country ; for during this period *general education* and the *building of places of worship* have been greatly promoted.

With respect to the diminished consumption of malt, the almost total disuse of domestic brewing amongst all classes, and the falling off in the *malt duties* of *more than a half* during the last three-quarters of a century, are facts so indisputable as only to need to be stated. That these results, placed in juxta-position with the recent strides of population, are in strict accordance with the theory here propounded, is to the author sufficiently apparent. Let us now see what the population of England is in proportion to its contents in square leagues. It will be found that these results accord with all that has been laid down as probable to vary that proportion either in one direction or another. It will be found to be less than the proportion in Ireland; less than in China; less than in the cultivated parts of Hindostan; but greater than in most other parts of Europe.

The area of England *approximates* to the contents of a triangle, the base of which is drawn from South Foreland in Kent to Land's-End in Cornwall. The sides by two lines commencing in these places, and meeting at Berwick-upon-Tweed. Of this figure the base is 340 miles : the eastern side 345 miles; the western side 425 miles. This, however, gives an area below the truth. A more minute calculation has determined that the area of England is 37,784,400 acres, or 59,053 British square miles. The result is as follows :—

ENGLAND.

Area in miles.	Population.	Persons to a square league.
59,053	14,000,000	2,118

It is to be observed, however, that the proportion of uncultivated land in England is less than in almost any country, and is believed not to exceed *ten millions of acres;* and that agriculture is carried to a high pitch of perfection.

In Scotland, where the greater part of the surface is absolutely barren, and from which a constant emigration goes on, the population is as high as *seven hundred persons* to the square league—an immense population for a country consisting principally of moor and mountain, and not much below that of the South of France, where all is fertility and beauty, and where the products of the soil grow almost spontaneously.

We now turn to the European Continent, where we shall find similar causes producing similar results. Looking first at the North of Germany, we shall find the food of the people poor, the country varied and often barren, and the population great. As we approach the richer provinces of Bavaria, and the regions nearer the Rhine, we shall find the population more moderate. When we examine those countries which are eminently rich and fertile, and where the *olive* forms a portion of the food of the people, as in Italy and France, we shall find the population lowest of all.

Taking Bohemia first of all, we see a region by no means naturally fertile and poorly cultivated, often mountainous, and of variable and cold climate. The principal food of the inhabitants consists of barley, oatmeal, potatoes, and milk ; even beer not being a general beverage, and for the most part reserved as a luxury for holidays —and what is the population ? The proportion to the *German square mile*, which is equal to about *twelve* British square miles, is no less than 3,885.

In Silesia, where the climate is much milder, the country fertile, and the corn crops greater, but the people poor and poorly fed, a similarly heavy population presents itself; the population to the *German square mile* being as high as 4,090. In Austria Proper, the greater part of which is much less fertile, the population is of course much below that of the fertile province of Silesia. It is, however, very high, amounting to no less than 2,837 persons to the *German square mile*. The poor, and for the most part, arid and barren kingdom of Prussia, affords results precisely similar. The kingdom is divided into Eastern and Western Prussia, and each of these divisions contains two Governments. The population is as follows :—

To the German mile.

		To the German mile.
Eastern Prussia.	Government of Koninsberg . . .	1,542
	Government of Gumbinnen . . .	1,495
Western Prussia.	Government of Dantzic	1,875
	Government of Mancsiwerden . .	1,244

4) 6,156

1,539 average.

A dense population for the most barren *level* country in Europe, and not much below that of the fertile and comparatively rich kingdom of Bavaria, the average population of which is 1,980 persons to the German square mile, according to M. Hassel's tables.

We now arrive at a country, the statistics of which are accurately known, and the results of which statistics strongly confirm the truth of this theory—that is to say, France. Of this, on the whole beautiful and great country, the climate and soil both vary, and we have on one side the rich vineyards, the smiling fields and fertile plains of Languedoc, and on the other the poor soil and harsher climate of Brittany. As soil and climate vary, so in some degree does the living of the people. In the South of France there is nothing but the appearance of ease and wealth. In the North we detect something more like the rags

and wretchedness of Ireland ; though in no part
of France is the food of the people reduced to
potatoes and a total absence of butchers' meat.
In no part of France is the poor peasant debarred
the use of the oil of the olive, the egg for his
omelette, the pullet for his pot, and occasionally
beef or mutton for his *soup* or *bouille*. As for
eggs, the quantity produced in France is prodigious. Of those imported into England, a
large portion comes from France; and the import
into England has amounted in a year to sixty-
nine millions, which at two-pence per dozen duty,
yielded £24,048. This was in 1836. Such being
the difference between the southern and the less
genial departments of France, the same differences
as to density of population which other countries
exhibit, are exhibited also here.

In the poorer Departments the population is
considerable. In the rich departments it is low.
At these results M. Malte Brun, who is one of
those writers who constantly regard a dense and
redundant population as evidence of the wealth
and industry of the country where it exists, without adverting to its causes, is sorely scandalised.
He rates the inhabitants of the South of France
for their dearth of children, which he terms
" poverty," though he admits that the country is

rich and fertile beyond description ; and not content with this even, is inclined to blame the *Government ;* though as to the means by which a Government could cure such an evil as this is, he affords no clue ! His observations are as follow :—

(*Malte Brun, Geography,* vol. viii. p. 273.)

" We have had occasion to observe the mild
" climate, the romantic sites, and the remains
" of Roman power in the twenty-eight Depart-
" ments that form the Southern region of France.
" The inhabitants, it has been seen, are favoured
" by nature : the different productions are admi-
" rably suited for their country : with the excep-
" tion of the mountains, the soil is everywhere
" fruitful. But if the population be compared
" with the surface, it will be found that the
" results accord ill with the natural advan-
" tages of the same vast region, which makes
" up more than a third part of the kingdom.
" The extent is equal to 9,000 square leagues,
" the population to 8,404,000 individuals ; thus,
" the number of inhabitants to every square
" league does not amount to *nine hundred and*
" *thirty-four*—a result below the mean number
" in the other divisions of the same country.

" Such facts are not without their value (*tres*
" *veritable*—M. Malte Brun): if the *best* and most
" fruitful part of France is comparatively *poor*
" and ill peopled, it proves how much the muni-
" ficence of Nature may be surpassed by the
" industry and resources of man. Government,
" too, may derive an important lesson from the
" same fact. It may thus be taught to appre-
" ciate the elements of its wealth and power.
" Thirteen Departments make up the Western
" region; the population relatively to the sur-
" face is greater than the last, for 5,423,000
" inhabitants are scattered over a surface of
" 4,200 French leagues; consequently the average
" number to every square league exceeds 1,290.
" Still the advantages of education are little
" known in the Western region: in that point
" it is almost on a level with the preceding.
" How much, then, might population and wealth
" be increased if ignorance no longer formed a
" barrier to the expansion of industry."

The truth is, that the really rich Departments
are the least populous, and the poorest most
populous—the riches in the one instance keeping down population, and the poverty in the
other instance urging it onwards. Let us con-

trast the poorest and the richest provinces of all
France, and the result will be strikingly apparent.
The poorest of the French provinces is unquestionably Bretagne, or Brittany.   It is described
by some travellers as reminding them of *Ireland*.
It accordingly presents all the indications of poor
living, squalor, rags, miserable habitations, multitudes of half-naked children, and numerous
mendicants or vagrants.   Let us see how Bretagne, or Brittany, stands with regard to population, and we shall find it giving what M. Malte
Brun would call "indications of industry and
wealth."   Strange infatuation !

POPULATION OF BRETAGNE, OR BRITTANY.

Departments.	Population to the square league.
1. Of Finisterre	1,376
2. . Coté du Nord	1,470
3. . Le Mortchan	1,157
4. . Isle de Vilaine	1,661
5. . Bas de Loire	1,405
	5) 7,069
Average to the square league . .	1,414

The richest province perhaps of France is
the beautiful province of Languedoc, with its
well-known salubrious towns of Montpellier and

Thoulouse. The climate is the finest probably
in Europe. The soil is excessively fertile, and
the vine and the olive vie with each other in
exuberance of fruit and beauty of growth. Here
is everything to sustain, to lengthen, and to
cherish life ; everything to afford plenty, ease,
and comfort to the inhabitants of this favoured
region. Yet, if we inquire into the numbers
of these inhabitants, we shall find them far below those of squalid, poor, and comparatively
sterile and inclement Brittany. And what is
the difference between them ? Wealth alone.
The laws, the language, and the people are the
same.

POPULATION OF THE PROVINCE OF LANGUEDOC.

Departments.	People to the square league.
1. Of Ardesche	1,120
2. . Aude	794
3. . Gard	1,103
4. . Herault	1,029
5. . Upper Garonne	1,153
6. . Upper Loire	1,105
7. . Lozere	521
8. . Tarn	1,083
	8) 7,908
Average to the square league . . .	988

The population, then, of the richest, or one of the richest of the French provinces, is not much more than two-thirds of that of the poorest, and thus will it ever be found, whether different countries, or different provinces of the same country, be compared with each other.

Italy is unquestionably, in fertility as well as climate, the finest country in Europe.

But where God has been most beneficent, man has been least so ; and as Italy, in natural advantages, is the finest, so, in regard to its government, it is the most unfortunate of European States—divided and subdivided amongst a variety of petty tyrants, all hating each other, and hated by their own subjects, industry is paralysed, trade almost destroyed, agriculture depressed, and universal languor prevailing throughout an idle and ignorant, or a vitiated and enervated population. Yet such is the natural wealth of the country, that, though afflicted with all these political evils, the Italians cannot, in point of comforts of living, be fairly said to be badly off, or in a state of suffering. There is much apparent poverty, much squalidity, but little starvation, in the proper sense of the word. Its condition is to be deduced clearly from its unfortunate political situation ; and under a good and united Government, no one doubts that Italy might be made one of the finest and happiest countries on earth. At present all is laziness, superstition, and debauchery: a political renovation would change this into activity and consequent wealth.

It is difficult to say what is the population of Italy as a whole. Looking, however, at the facts, as shown in the different States, it is not great, considering the immense advantages of the country, which is a natural garden throughout. It is quite certain that Italy could produce food for many more inhabitants than are now, or probably ever were, congregated upon her soil.

The Lombard-Venetian kingdom is one of the most populous portions of Italy. It contains the great trading mart of Venice, and many of the Universities—Milan, Pavia, Padua, &c. ; and has been, therefore, more liable to increase by immigration than many other provinces. Its people are, however, by no means numerous, when compared with the surface, that surface being of unrivalled fertility, and under a climate the most delicious.

The following table shows the proportion to the *geographical square league*, which, it must be remembered, is about *one-seventh larger* than the ordinary square league :---

LOMBARD-VENETIAN KINGDOM.

Square geographical leagues.	Population.	Persons to the league.
2,368	2,237,301	1,840

This, when the difference of the geographical league is taken, is a population a little above the average of France. This, however, is far above that of most of the other States; indeed, above that of all the extended States. *Lucca, San Marino,* and *Massa,* are little more than *towns,* with a small territory, and not States. The next great territory is that of the Church. Its population is shown in the following table:

STATES OF THE CHURCH.

Square geographical leagues.	Population.	Persons to the league.
2,257	2,590,000	1,147

The next great territory is the Duchy of Tuscany. This fine country contains the beautiful cities of Florence and of Pisa, and the port of Leghorn. Its population is as follows:---

GREAT DUCHY OF TUSCANY.

Surface in geographical sq. leagues.	Population, 1826.	Persons to each league.
1,098	1,275,000	1,161.

The dominions of the King of Sardinia, including Piedmont and the Island of Sardinia, is much more scanty. The two give the following results :—

PIEDMONT.

Area in geographical sq. leagues.	Population.	Persons to each league.
2,635	3,399,600	1,260

ISLAND OF SARDINIA.

Area in geographical sq. leagues.	Population.	Persons to the league.
1,100	490,087	445

The island abounds in cattle, some of which only are domesticated, the rest running half wild over the mountainous part of the island. This is the case not only with horned cattle, but with the swine and even with the horses. The cattle upon the whole are supposed to be three times as numerous as the inhabitants.

The population of the Duchies of Parma and of Modina give similar results :—

PARMA.

Area in geographical square leagues.	Population.	To the league.
288	440,000	1,180

MODENA.

Area in geographical square leagues.	Population.	To the league.
260	350,000	1,346

Such is the truth as to the population of the fine and rich countries of France and of Italy, and such is the state of the population in all

countries where the vine and the olive abound
and where the juice of the grape and the rich
oil of the olive form a portion of the daily food
of the people, together with such animal food as
they can procure, or are in the habit of using.
Spain and Portugal being mountainous countries,
and also countries where grazing is practised in
a large proportion, as compared with agriculture,
are still more thinly peopled.

SPAIN.

Area in square French leagues.	Population.	Persons to the league.
23,867	13,901,000	580

PORTUGAL.

Area in square French leagues.	Population.	Persons to the league.
4,922	3,214,000	653

In Italy it has been ascertained that the
average number of births to a marriage are
three only, a low proportion, and below that of
almost any other country—*Southern France*,
perhaps, excepted.

We now turn to a country less favoured than the foregoing as to climate, but fertile in a high degree, and cultivated with great care---Holland and Belgium—as constituting the former kingdom of the Netherlands. Of these countries it may be said, that as Italy is the *natural*, so they are the *artificial*, garden of Europe. Destitute of mountains or even hills, they present one vast plain, covered with alternate arable land, and meadow and pasture of inexpressible richness. The vine is cultivated, but the wine made from its fruit is indifferent ; wheaten bread, milk, cheese, and animal food, are the nutriment of the people ; with such a proportion of esculent vegetables as they themselves choose to add. Malt liquor is also in use, as well as the less wholesome distillation from grain, to which the country gives its name. The population of this wealthy country is, as nearly as possible, one person to each *hectare* of land. This, in English measure, is about *two hundred* to the square mile, or *eighteen hundred to the square British league only ;* and this in a tract, every foot of which is under culture. The number of births to a marriage are *four* upon the average, with a fraction more. Immigration here has done much to swell the population. The great trading marts of Holland are filled with strangers. In Belgium also foreign settlers are numerous, yet such are the results.

Looking next at the countries in the North of Europe, that is to say, at Denmark and Sweden, we find the same law apparent. Both are grazing countries more than agricultural, and in both the population is moderate, making proper allowance for the mountainous tracts which prevail in both. In Sweden, it has been proved by the Tables of Mortality that the population *decreased* rather than increased down to the year 1763. Since that time agriculture has been pushed, to the exclusion of grazing cattle, especially in Gothland, and there the population has increased decidedly since 1763.

In Denmark, agriculture is more prevalent than in Sweden, and less animal food eaten upon the whole; the population, however, is moderate, being *six hundred and seventy-seven only to the square league.*

Turning next to the Continent of America, we shall find the same law evidently prevailing. In the Brazils and Mexico, where cattle are a large part of the wealth of the country, the population is thin and scattered. Nor is the rapid increase of the United States any difficulty, though much stress has been laid upon it. That it is the result of a constant immigration into that favoured land from all the European countries is sufficiently evident; and this may be proved by a comparison of the number of marriages and births in those towns where emigrants in great numbers do not resort, when it will be found that the increase is little or nothing. Thus, in Portsmouth, the capital town of New Hampshire, and *not* a rich town, the returns are as follow :---

	Marriages.	Births.	Proportion to a Marriage.
1804 to 1809.	381	1,702	4 and a fraction.

The return for the *rich* city of Philadelphia shows thus :---

	Marriages.	Births.	Proportion to a Marriage.
A. D. 1818.	792	2,221	(Less than) 3.

In addition to this, taking from Mr. Barbour's publication the ratio of population for the little parish of Hingham Massachusets, the result is nearly the same. In fifty-four years there were

2,247 births, 1,113 deaths, and 521 marriages
This makes the proportion of births less than
four to each marriage, from which must be deducted a large portion of the deaths. Looking
at the results of the general American census
both for 1800 and 1810 (before immigration was
so extensive), it appears that the number of
adults above sixteen years of age was equal to
the number of children below that age ; which,
as Mr. Godwin observes, "shows no rapid
increase by procreation ; as, if so, the children
ought to have *far outnumbered* the adults." On
the other hand, it is evident enough, surely, and
needing little reflection, to see, that in a country
where *sixty thousand emigrants enter one port
alone in a year* (New York), the progress of
population must, from that cause alone, be
rapid indeed !

Upon a review of the whole statistical details
of this chapter, the results appear to be so
striking that it is difficult to avoid the conclusion, that as the food of a people degenerates
from a preponderance of animal nutriment to a
vegetable diet, in that *ratio* the population increases and thickens ; and that, as this description of aliment is still reduced lower, first, by the
denial of all animal food ; next, by the denial or

the products of the olive and the vine; and, lastly, by the change from a wheaten or barley diet to one consisting chiefly of rice, or of the potatoe---in that same *ratio* will the population still go on increasing and thickening, until it has reached the verge of constant starvation, and is perpetually thinned by periodical famines and epidemic fevers, the certain consequences of this state. Nor does it appear to make any difference whether this mode of living is induced by climate naturally, as is perhaps the case in certain countries, or artificially by superstition, or by the relative position of one part of society to that of another part, as is perhaps the case in other countries. Thus, we see the most dense and redundant population in those immense regions, comprehended under the term China, in Japan, and generally throughout the peninsula of Hindostan, where the climate has almost forced the natives upon a vegetable diet and upon the cultivation of rice almost solely, and where superstition has completed what the climate probably originated. Next to this in density, however, we find the population of Ireland---which is essentially and naturally a pastoral country, and where, were it not for an artificial and depraved state of society, which has gradually compelled the mass of the inhabitants to a poor manner of sustenance, not arising out of any necessity of soil and climate, the population would have been moderate instead of redundant, and wealthy instead of poor.

Nor, as it seems to the author, is there the slightest difficulty in accounting for the growth of the population of the United States of America, if the circumstances of the last sixty years be impartially considered with a view to this question. It is true that, generally speaking, the circumstances in which the inhabitants of the older and more settled portions of these regions are placed do not conduce to rapid increase ; and we have seen accordingly, that, looking at the statistics of such towns as have not been much subjected to the effects of immigration, the increase has not been great, nor anything beyond what might be expected, under the peculiar views of the phenomena of population now brought forward. To account for the population of the Republic of the United States, we must look first to their importation of Negro slaves, which went on throughout the Southern States during the whole period of their colonial existence ; next, to the emigration from the Mother Country to the Colonies, which was always in operation to a greater or less extent;

and lastly, to the increased emigration which has, during the sixty years of their independence, been flowing into the territories of the Republic from almost every country in Europe. In addition to the natural increase of the earlier settlers in Virginia, the Carolinas, and the Southern Planting States, a large coloured population has gradually been created, originating in the commerce between the convicts and other European races and the Negroes; and to this source of increase the influx of new free English and Irish settlers was constantly adding another and healthier cause of progress in numbers. At the time of the declaration of Independence, it was believed that the Republic contained fully three millions of persons, of all ages. If we calculate the effects of the constant immigration into the States, which has gone on throughout the whole sixty years that have elapsed since the conclusion of the American struggle, we shall find no cause to wonder that the numbers of the Republic have risen to their present amount. Taking the immigration drawn into all the States from all parts of the world in a lump—English, Irish, Scotch, Germans, Dutch, Mexican Spaniards, and Frenchmen, not forgetting Jews, we can hardly exceed in taking an average of thirty

thousand persons per annum. This alone is an
addition of a million and three quarters, one half
of whom may be still living. When, however, it
is considered that these emigrants nearly altogether consist of young persons, adults, of both
sexes, and that they may be safely held to be
placed under circumstances which would render
them both desirous and fully capable of immediately and rather rapidly adding to their numbers,
all wonder ceases, for the stimulus to population
in such a case is easily seen to be enormous.
The persons emigrating are nearly altogether of
that class, where fecundity is rendered certain
by circumstances—young men and women in the
prime of life, in full health, having suffered probably some privations, and generally driven by
narrow circumstances, and a hope of bettering
their condition, to seek an active life of enterprise and industry, with scanty means ; but in
a bountiful, plentiful, and rich country. In a
condition like this, each year of emigration would
be felt not only in its mere addition, but in an
immediate increase by propagation, stretching
probably over the next ten years, or next fifteen
years. Repeat this year after year, at the average rate assumed, or at a rate much below that,
and the reduplication will be found to be enor-

mous. With these observations the author leaves this division of his subject in the hands of his readers.

Upon the whole of the foregoing considerations, as detailed in all the preceding chapters, it can hardly be denied that we have now arrived at the proof of a high probability that the theory of population, which it is the aim of the present treatise to establish, is true. Examining, in the first place, the causes of the increase or decrease of limited bodies of men, of whose peculiar mode of living we have the means of obtaining indubitable general information, it appears to be clearly made out, that, wherever such men are kept in the plethoric state, they cannot keep up their own numbers, much less increase and multiply. On the other hand, it seems equally clear, that, in the instances in which a great increase has taken place, which, be it observed, are rare, this increase has invariably arisen out of a state of depletion, hardship, or low feeding. This is the state of the evidence as far as it has been practicable to collect it with regard to limited numbers of persons, with the routine of whose lives we have the means of being generally acquainted : in the statistics of nations the same law of Nature is equally and beautifully manifest.

Going through the principal nations of the
globe, of which we can be said to possess anything like intimate knowledge, we trace the same
law through all its varieties as accompanied and
caused by the variations in the mode of living,
arising out of the difference of climate, civilization, and religion. Beginning with those countries in which the pastoral life, and subsistence
by the feeding of cattle, form the characteristic of
the people, we find the population thin in the
extreme, as in the grazing portions of the Russian
empire, and those other countries where either
soil or climate, or the customs of the inhabitants,
or all three, discourage agriculture and tillage,
and tend to the production of animal food.
Passing from these to countries and nations
where tillage and the growth of edible grain are
mingled with the breeding and grazing of cattle,
we see a uniform and most marked increase in
the population, as measured by the square league
or mile; but we still see the population within
bounds, and far below that of those countries in
which a food, scanty in itself, and almost wholly
vegetable, prevails. In many of those hotter
climates, also, where the effect of the burning sun
upon the herbage is such as naturally to check
in a great measure the fattening of sheep or

oxen, we discover that the deficiency of rich food is made up, *first*, by the peculiar fruits which encourage the breeding of swine and of poultry; and, *secondly*, by the rich and oleaginous species of nourishment afforded to the nature of such regions by the fruits themselves which are peculiar to the climate. Thus, in Spain, in France, in Italy, and in Portugal, though the fattening of oxen and sheep is less easy than in the more temperate climates, yet the immense quantities of poultry and of swine, and also the use of the rich and luxurious products of the olive and the vine, make amends for the partial deficiency of animal food. In these countries the produce of domestic fowls, and consequently of eggs, is known to be enormous, as indeed the extraordinary quantity of the latter imported from France and Belgium into this country amply proves; and if to this we add the constant use of olive oil and of wine as articles of daily diet, we shall easily perceive that, though the fat beeves of more temperate countries are wanting, there is yet no want of rich nutriment to the inhabitants, nor of plenty of means to maintain that plethoric state of the frame which seems necessary to moderate the prolificness of all animals, man not excepted. Carrying round our gaze from one part of the globe to another, we at length discover that enormous population is attendant only upon a nutriment totally vegetable, and of the thinnest and poorest kind, and that not in abundance, but the contrary. We find enormous swarms of mankind covering certain regions : we mark these phenomena in Hindostan, in China, in Japan, and latterly in Ireland ; and on inquiry we find that these people are destitute of the olive and the vine; and not knowing what the taste of animal food is, subsist for the most part upon the inunctuous fruits, upon fish, and the less farinaceous grain and roots—upon the products of the sea and rivers, upon rice, upon tea, upon the potato, and upon the more acid descriptions of fruit.

Thus far, then, viewing the effects of diet upon all practicable scales—viewing them as exhibited in the condition of nations as well as of small bodies of men—we perceive the same laws manifesting themselves throughout, in all their various degrees and modifications, shade following shade. We see luxury not only forbidding increase, but causing rapid decrease ; we see a more moderate, but still a gross and luxurious mode of subsistence, producing the like effects in a mitigated way. Going further down the scale,

we find an imperfect supply of nutriment immediately followed, and always accompanied, by an
increase of fecundity and numbers; and, whenever we see this applied to an entire population,
we witness rapid increase, and all the fearful
effects of over-population going on together with
increasing pressure.

CHAPTER VI.

MINOR PROOFS NOT INCLUDED IN THE FOREGOING
CHAPTERS.

In prosecuting an inquiry like the present, it
will always be found that there are minor facts
and arguments bearing quite directly upon the
question at issue, but which cannot easily be
classed under any general head, or so managed
as to be made a part of the main stream of the
argument. Of some of these, which though they
go directly, and, it is hoped, strongly, to prove
the truth of the law regulating population here
attempted to be established, are yet in their
nature insulated and distinct, it is now intended
to treat.

In the first place, it may be remarked, as a
proof of the continual care taken by Nature to
preserve the species, that, though the prolific
state may have apparently ceased for many

years, yet immediately preceding its real and
actual cessation, offspring, as a last effort, are
very frequently produced; and hence, just as
fruit-trees, on the year before they die, commonly bear a large crop of fruit; so women,
frequently, who have been unprolific for many
years, bear a child, many frequently twins,
towards their advanced age. Upon this, as a
fact familiar to all medical persons and physiologists, it is needless to insist further. Another
striking corroboration of the law here endeavoured
to be established, is the fact, that childless
couples, who have been accustomed to full and
luxurious living, very frequently have children
after being reduced in their circumstances, and
unable to live as before. Of this undoubted
fact every reader almost will, in his or her own
experience, be able to point out examples; and
therefore it would be useless to dilate upon it.
The constant occurrence of the fact, however, and
its causes, may be shown in a different manner—it
being a truth quite capable of proof upon an
extended scale, that prolificness always is a
concomitant of a change in the mode of living
from plenty to the contrary. It was probably
from this being the case, that the observation
took its rise, which asserts that " more children

are born in winter than in summer !" A
singular remark, but not devoid of truth—applied,
as it no doubt was, to Catholic countries. The
cause is stated by Swift in one of his humorous
allusions, as follows:—" We are told (says he)
" by a grave author, an eminent French physician,
" that fish being a prolific diet, there are more
" children born in Roman Catholic countries
" about nine months after Lent, than at any
" other season." Now, although this is quoted
by Swift in one of his ironical Treatises—(" A
Modest Proposal to the Publick for preventing
the Children of the Poor being a Burthen to their
Parents."—*vide* Swift's Works, vol. ix.)—there
is no reason to suppose that fact has not been
observed ; and Lent falling always in Spring, the
origin of the proverb as to the increase of births
in winter is evident enough. The observation
of the French physician is, in truth, only a repe-
tition of the ancient notion as to a diet on fish
being a cause of prolificness ; which no question
it is—not because the diet is *fish*, but because the
diet is *poor*. The best proof, however, that
seasons of scarcity and seasons of prolificness are
almost synonimous terms, is supplied by the late
Michael Thomas Sadler, in his work on Population. In volume ii. of that work, he has con-

structed, amidst many others, the following tables, which certainly, if ever anything was demonstrated, demonstrate this beyond a doubt. The wonder is how the acute mind of Mr. Sadler could contemplate these results, without being led by them to discover what is really the law by which population is regulated. His failing to do this, is only one more example of how apt preconceived theories are apt to distort views of evidence, even in the strongest minds. As a contradiction of the theory of Mr. Malthus – whose views Mr. Sadler was eager to combat—the results, as stated by him, are conclusive and invaluable. As a help to his own theory, they are quite nugatory. With the views of this question, now attempted to be established, they perfectly accord. Mr. Sadler, it will be seen, has taken three separate instances of years of plenty, either following or preceding years of scarcity ; and by taking the births through a certain consequent period after both years, the result is, in all, that the conceptions in the years of dearth exceed those of the plentiful years, although the marriages of the years of plenty, are, as might be expected, for the most part, more than those of the years of pressure. In each of the years compared, the number of marriages and conceptions,

and the prices of wheat are given: the reader
will remark how very curiously the results
correspond.

In the first Table, No. 1, the year of scarcity
precedes that of plenty. The marriages of the
year of dearth are, very naturally, much fewer
than those of the plentiful year, and yet the
conceptions are more ; thus shewing that an
increase in the means of comfortable and full
living, immediately *checks* population.

TABLE, No. 1.

Years.	Marriages.	Conceptions.	Price of Wheat.
			£ s. d.
1796	73,107	268,088	3 17 1
1798	79,477	266,769	2 10 3
Difference	+ 6,370	— 1,319	1 6 10

In the next Table, No. 2, the year of plenty
comes first, and is a precursor to that of dearth.
In the year of dearth, it will be seen there is a
striking diminution in the number of marriages.
They fall off by a whole *eighth*. Despite of this,
however, there is great increase of conceptions,
amounting nearly to a twelfth additional ; thus

proving that a diminution of the means of living comfortably immediately *stimulates* population.

TABLE, No. 2.

Years.	Marriages.	Conceptions.	Price of Wheat.
			£ *s. d.*
1799	77,557	254,870	3 7 6
1801	67,228	273,837	5 18 3
Difference	— 10,329	+ 18,967	+ 2 10 9

In the Table, No. 3, the year of comparative plenty again comes first; and in the year of dearth the marriages again diminish in number, though not in the ratio of the preceding table. The extraordinary part of this table is, however, the proof which it affords, that the conceptions accurately correspond with the prices of food. In this table the lowest price of wheat, *sixty-one shillings and tenpence the quarter*, is really a high price. According to this theory, then, the stimulus to population is already in activity; and the conclusion, *a priori*, is, that an enhanced price ought not to be followed by an effect proportionately as great as would have been, or ought to have been, the case had the advance

of price been from a lower average. This, it will
be observed, is completely borne out in the result.
The conceptions do increase, notwithstanding
the diminution of marriages; but in a ratio far
below that of the former tables, where the
starting point is from actual cheapness to dearness. The value of this result, as confirming
the truth of the views now attempted to be
established, must be evident to everybody.

TABLE, No. 3.

Years.	Marriages.	Conceptions.	Price of Wheat.
			£ s. d.
1815	99,944	330,199	3 1 10
1817	88,234	331,384	4 10 7
Difference	— 11,710	+ 1,185	+ 1 8 9

To the above tables it is hardly necessary to add
any further remarks. They strongly prove the
pervading description of the law of Nature, that
any diminution of means which tends to endan-
ger the species is immediately met by an increased sexual fertility. It may, however, be
proper to observe, that the existence of this
beautiful law of Providence is also proved by

the admitted facts of the rapidity with which gaps in a population, caused by plague, or other pestilential visitations, are filled up ; and of the immensely increased tendencies to propagation which medical persons testify are always exhibited by persons recovering from plague, typhus, and other contagious disorders.

Suffering the foregoing considerations to rest, as all such considerations must rest, upon the good old rule of " valeant, quantum valere possunt," there is yet another proof to be adduced of the validity of the reasoning which they embody, and this of a nature at variance with all existing theories of population, and the maxims founded upon them. It has very generally and very plausibly been set down as an obvious truth, that " late marriages " are a " check to population;" and if carried far enough, with regard to the important point of delay, there can be no doubt that this is not only a truth, but a truism. Provident Nature has, however, done all she could to secure the continuation of the species against this danger ; and singular to relate, but most indubitably true it is, that when marriage is delayed, fertility is increased, in the *ratio* of delay, until the point is passed after which the bearing of children becomes impossible. In order to prove this extra-ordinary and very instructive fact, the following table is adduced. It was constructed by Doctor Granville, and Mr. Finlayson, the well-known accountant, and is based upon the particulars of *eight hundred and seventy-six cases,* which that eminent practitioner attended as " Physician to the Benevolent Lying-In Institution, and West-minster Dispensary." It will be observed that the cases were, in all human probability, those of females in the same station of life ; all pro-bably suckling their own children, and exposed to none of the causes of partial sterility on one hand, or stimulated fertility on the other, to which females in the more artificial stations of life are subjected.

TABLE.

SHOWING THE EFFECT THAT THE POSTPONEMENT OF MARRIAGE IN FEMALES HAS UPON THEIR ANNUAL FECUNDITY.

Ages when married.	Average of births to the year.
13 to 16	·456,706
16 .. 20	·503,610
21 .. 24	·520,227
25 .. 28	·545,163
29 .. 32	·589,811
33 .. 36	·776,866
37 .. 39	1·125,000

The results in the above table are given in decimals; but the general results may be described as follows :—When females marry at, or before twenty years of age, their. average offspring is not quite a child in two years. From twenty to thirty-two, females marrying produce on an average somewhat faster than a child in two years. If married from thirty-three to thirty-six years of age, females will average more than two births in three years; and from thirty-seven to thirty-nine, about a birth in each eleven months, being rather more than one each year.

All these results, it may be safely affirmed, tend one way. That is to say, they go directly to confirm the existence of that great natural law which provides that the power of increase shall itself grow with the exigencies of the occasion; and that, as the continuation of the species may be endangered, in that exact proportion the facility and power of continuance shall be enlarged and extended. That this law extends to the human race, as well as being the regulator of the fecundity and produce both of the inferior animals and the vegetable kingdom, seems to be abundantly clear, as far as the proofs derived directly from physiology as well as statistics are concerned. There are, however,

of course, other and more circuitous roads by
which we may arrive at other proofs, and to the
same conclusions ; and to these the natural
course and current of the argument next incline
us to turn.

CHAPTER VII.

ARGUMENT FROM THE SOLUTION OF SOME HISTORICAL DIFFICULTIES.

In the treatment of a subject like that under review, in addition to the more direct arguments on which the proofs needed are to rest and be embodied, there are also evidences of an indirect kind, which though perhaps not of themselves conclusive as to the issue, are yet, if joined to other and more simple evidence, strongly corroborative of the truth which, upon the whole, is sought to be established. If, for instance, we can point out one or more historical facts, undoubted as facts, but of which a satisfactory explanation has never been given; and if the theory as to population, and the laws which regulate it, which is now sought to be established, shall afford an easy, natural, and self-evident

explanation of these heretofore historical puzzles
or mysteries, than this solution, so arrived at,
though not in itself a direct evidence that the
theory itself *is* true, is yet presumptive evidence
that it probably *may be true;* and if this presumptive proof is corroborated by direct proof, then
is the argument upon the whole strengthened by
such coincidences; the direct and the indirect
testimonies mutually confirming each other.
That there are more than one historical fact of
this inexplicable nature, but which, admitting the
theory now treated of to be true, are rendered
easily explicable, it is the business of this chapter
to show; and it is hoped that the few preliminary
remarks which he has thought it proper to make
will avail to show that no improper weight is
intended by the author to be laid upon testimony
of this kind; and that this part of the argument,
though strictly logical as intended to be applied,
is given likewise as a matter of curiosity, as it
bears, in the reflex, upon the historical points
in question.

The first point to which the author would
advert occurs in the history of his own country.
It is that decay in population which was supposed
to have been in progress from about the year
fourteen hundred and eighty-eight, up to a period

probably ending about sixteen hundred and fifty ; that is to say, from the commencement of Henry the Seventh's reign up to that of Charles the Second. That such a decay was supposed by those living at the time to be going on, is a fact quite unquestionable. It may be proved not only from the writers of the period, but from the Statute Book, where it is not only frequently alluded to, but where it forms the subject of one or more actual and entire statutes. The most remarkable circumstance, however, is, that this decay of population, real or supposed, singular as it may seem in itself, went on in company with increasing luxury for the greater portion of the time, on the part of the whole people, and especially on the part of the labouring people. Nor is there the slightest reason to suppose that during any part of the period, save and except during some years of the reign of Queen Elizabeth, anything like want existed, in any extended sense, anywhere in England ; and of this not only the writings of the time, but the Statute Book also, affords proof in abundance.

Let us now look at the evidence of the first of these facts, that is to say, of the general belief of a decay of the people which prevailed at the period referred to. That such a belief existed, no man who has looked at the Statutes of these remote periods can doubt. Sir Frederick M. Eden, in his " History of the state of the Poor," (vol. 1, p. 73,) says, " from 1488, and for a century and a half after this period, DEPOPULATION continued to be the theme of the Legislature !" That this assertion of Sir Frederick Eden is founded on truth and actual facts, a very cursory inspection of the Acts passed during the period he refers to, and during the periods of about half a century before and after, will afford sufficient testimony to the inquirer. The strongest proof of the evident decay in population, as evinced by " the pulling down of houses and towns," is perhaps the Statute of the fourth year of Henry VII., chapter 19. This act, it will be seen, after asserting and describing the decay of houses all over the country, especially in the agricultural parts, where changes in trade do not shift or draw together masses of people, absolutely empowers the authorities to repair any ruinous house, which shall have twenty or more acres of land attached, out of the rents, without or against the owner's consent, and levies heavy penalties for neglect of the provisions of such statute.

The following Extract will, in some measure, put the reader in possession of the intent as well as the grounds of this extraordinary Act, which prove incontestibly the RAPID DECAY of population at the time of its enactment, though the remedies proposed be inapplicable and absurd. The Act itself extends over many folio pages, and is extremely rare. That its great length has been one cause of its exclusion from the ordinary editions of the Statutes is probable ; but it is also quite as likely, that the singular nature of its preamble and enactments must have contributed to its banishment from all modern collections of Acts of Parliament. Under the views we are at this time accustomed to take of the subject of population, the whole seems an inexplicable farrago, and more like a hallucination of Legislative insanity, than an enactment of sane men. The theory, however, now in course of being proved, affords a key to the whole mystery ; and the causes which no doubt influenced the Legisture are at once apparent and certain.

CHAPTER 19th, HENRY 7th—Anno Quarto.

The penalty for decaying of Houses of Husbandry, or not laying of convenient Land for the maintenance of the same.

Item, the King our Soueraigne Lord, having a singular pleasure above all things to avoide such enormities and mischiefes, as be hurtfull and pre-judiciall to the common weale of this his land and his subiects of the same, remembreth that, among all other things great inconveniences daily doe increase, by desolation and pulling downe and wilfull waste of houses and towns within this Realme, and laying to pasture lands, which customably have beene used in tillage, whereby idlenesse, which is the ground off, and beginning of all mischiefes, daily doth encrease.

For where in some towns two hundred persons were occupied and lieued by their lawfull labours, now there are occupied two or three heardmen, and the residue fall into idlenesse, the husbandrie which is one of the greatest commodities of this Realme, is greatly decayed, Churches destroyed, the service of God withdrawen, the bodies there buried not prayed for, the Patrons and Curates wronged, the defence of this land against our enemies outward, feebled and impaired, to the great displeasure of God, to the subuersion of the pollicie of, and good rule of this land, if remidie be not provided : Wherefore the King our Soueraigne Lord, by the advice of the Lords spirituall and temporall, and the commons of this said Parliament assembled, and by authority of the same, hath ordained, enacted, and stablished, that no person, of what estate, degree, or condition that he be, that hath any house or houses, that at any time within three years past, hath beene or that now is, or that hereafter shall be lette for ferme, with xx. (20) acres of land at least, or more, lying in tillage and husbandrie, that the owner or owners of every such house or houses, or land, doe keepe, sustaine, maintaine houses and buildings vpon the said ground, and land convenient and necessarie for maintaining and vpholding of the said tillage and husbandrie.

And if any such owners or owner of any such houses, or houses and land, take land and occupie any such house or houses, and keep in his or their owne hands, that the saide owner or owners, by the saide authoritie be bound in likewise to keepe and maintaine houses vpon the saide ground and land, convenient and necessarie for the maintaining and vpholding of the saide tillage and husbandrie. And if any man doe contrary to the premisses of any of them, that then it be lawfull to the King, if any such lands or houses be holden of him immediately, or to the Lords of the Fees, if if any such lands be holden of them immediately, to receive yeerely halfe the value of the issues and profits of any such lands, whereof the house or houses be not so maintained and sustained. And the same half deale of the issues and profits to have, holde, and keepe to his or their own vse, without anything therefore to be payed or given, till such time as the same house or houses bee sufficiently builded or repaired againe. And that no manner of freehold be in the King, nor any such Lord or Lords, by the taking of any such profits, of or in any such lands in no manner of forme: but onely the King, and the saide Lord or Lords, have power to take, receive, and have the saide issues and profits, as is above saide, and therefore the King, or the saide Lord or Lords to have power to distraine for the saide issues and profits, to be had and perceived by them, in forme above sayde, by authoritie of this present Acte.

This Act is, however, borne most amply out by many others, which demonstrate that the decay which caused all this alarm extended into boroughs and cities, as well as rural villages and townships. Thus the Act of the third year of the next reign (Henry VIII.), chapter 8, recites in the preamble, that "MANY, and the MOST PART, of *cities, boroughs,* and *towns corporate,* be fallen to ruin and decay." That this decay of houses followed a progressive diminution of the population, the statutes of the same period prove. Thus, in another Act of the fourth year of Henry the Seventh, being chapter 16, it is asserted, that there is "a great decay of people in the Isle of Wight." This Act was passed in the year 1488, referred to by Sir Frederick Morton Eden, as the time when the alarm of "depopulation" begins to be evident in the Statute Book. It is a most preposterous mode of argument to endeavour to throw doubts upon the facts, because, up to this period, no one has had any true knowledge of the causes. They will neither admit of denial nor of being explained away. It will not do to say that the population were, by the operations of trade, drawn into the towns; because we see that the decay was equally evident in the cities, boroughs, and towns, in spite of any tendency of the people to draw to the towns, a tendency which to some extent certainly did exist; and the causes of which shall be pointed out afterwards, existing, as they do, in that same Statute Book which describes the diminution of the numbers of the people. As might be expected from persons legislating in profound ignorance of the *real* causes of the phenomena, which they could not help seeing, the causes *assigned*, and the remedies prescribed in these Acts, are highly absurd. "Monopoly" was the bugbear mostly relied on by the alarmists, and the consolidation of farms, and monopolies of live-stock, and different trading monopolies, are inveighed against and limited by various Acts, which fix a maximum of the acres, cattle and sheep, apprentices, &c. &c., to be occupied, or owned, or employed, by the individual. These laws were doubtless sufficiently absurd and impracticable; but they afford proof indubitable of the existence of the state of things which they were intended to remedy.

Such being the facts as to the state of the population during the period of English history referred to, it next remains to be shown that this decay of towns and their inhabitants cannot be explained upon any hypothesis built upon any supposed law of population hitherto attempted to be established. Upon such theories as those which depend upon the assertion that exuberance of food stimulates population, the extraordinary facts alluded to by Sir Frederick Morton Eden must be held to be absolutely preternatural; for, during the entire period throughout which they manifested themselves, it may be proved beyond the possibility of a doubt, that luxury amongst the middling, and exuberant plenty amongst the very lowest classes, universally prevailed. Of this truth there is not only copious, but various proof. Not only do the writers of the time describe, in a way not to be misunderstood, the amazing ease and plenty which then prevailed throughout England, but the Statutes of the period teem with testimonies of a similar sort. These statutary proofs are of more than one sort. *First*, there are Acts distinctly against luxury of certain sorts; *next*, there are Acts to limit the wages of labour and keep down luxuriousness of living amongst the people at large; and, *lastly*, there are statutes which, in their preamble, describe the plenty then existing. It is necessary for the purposes of this argument to advert to all these in detail, and in their turn, taking them, as nearly as possible, in the order in which they are now mentioned. First, as to the writers.

Of the few writers touching upon the subject in question who flourished at the early periods now referred to, the highest in point of authority stands probably Chief Justice Sir John Fortescue. His celebrated treatise, " De Laudibus Legum Angliæ," contains evidence the most indubitable of the flourishing state in which England was at the era when it was written. This evidence is the more incontestibly strong, because it is in some degree indirect. Fortescue was not, intentionally, writing a statistical statement of the

wealth and mode of living of the English people
— quite the contrary.   His book is a book of
law, and the intention of the learned and vene-
rable writer was to exalt the law and constitutional Government of England above those
of other countries.   In order to do this effectually, he compares the well-known state of the
English people, at the time of his writing, with
that of the people of France, where he then was
as guardian to the Prince, the eldest son of
Henry VI. (afterwards killed at Tewkesbury,)
during the civil wars of Lancaster and York;
and he deduces the wealth and ease of the one,
compared with the poverty and wretchedness
of the other, from the comparative perfection
and imperfection of the laws under which each
lived.   This part of Chief Justice Fortescue's
book is, therefore, an appeal to facts notorious
to the world, in corroboration of a legal argument; and, as such, it becomes the best possible
evidence of the state and condition of the English
people at the time when its distinguished author
wrote.   The following passages contain invaluable testimony of the wealth, independence,
ease, and comfort, which existed in England
when they were written.   Under the head entitled, " Why inquests are not made by juries

of twelve men in other realms as well as in England?" Fortescue thus writes:—

" Moreover, the same countrie is so filled and
" replenished with landed men, that therein so
" small a thorp cannot be found wherein dwelleth
" not a Knight or Esquire, or such a householder
" as is there commonly called a Franchelayne,
" enriched with great possessions; and also other
" freeholders (*libere tenentes*) and many yeomen
" (*valecti*), able for their livelihoods to make a
" jury in form aforementioned; for there be in
" that land divers yeomen which are able to
" dispend by the year above a hundred pounds
" (*sexcenta scuta*), (i. e., *a hundred pounds of the*
" *money of Selden's time*, 1640 *to* 1650, *when*
" *he translated Fortescue; probably six times or*
" *seven times the value of the money of the*
" *present time.*) Wherefore juries, afore-declared,
" are then very oft made, specially in great
" matters, of Knights and Esquires, and others
" whose possessions, in the whole, amounteth
" yearly above the sum of five hundred marks
" (*duo millia scutorum*). Wherefore it cannot
" be thought that such men can be suborned, or
" that they will be perjured; not only for that
" they have before their eyes the fear of God,
" but also for that they have a careful regard

" to the preservation of their honours, and to
" the eschewing of reproach or dammage there-
" upon ensueing, and also that their heirs be not
" impeached through their infamie. After this
" manner, O mighty Prince, are none other
" realms of the world disposed and inhabited !"—
Fortescue de Laudibus, p. 65, chapter 49.

Under the head of " the Commodities that
proceed of the joint Government Politique and
Royal in the Realm of England," he proceeds
thus : —

" Hereby it cometh to passe that the men of
" this land are riche, having abundance of gold
" and silver, and (all) other things (*cunctis*
" *necessariis*) for the maintenance of man's life.
" They drink no water, unlesse it be so that
" some for devotion and upon a zeale of pe-
" nance do abstain from other drink. They eat
" plentifully of all kinds of flesh and fish. They
" weare fine woollen cloth in their apparell.
" They have also abundance of bed-coverings
" in their houses and of all other woollen stuffe,
" they have great store of all hustlements (*hos-
" lilimentis)* and implements of household. They
" are plentifully furnished with all instruments
" of husbandry, and with all other things that
" are requisite to the accomplishment of a quiet

" and wealthy life according to their estates and " degrees."—*Fortescue de Laudibus*, page 85, chapter 36.

Here we have a description of national wealth and comfort unmatchable, as Sir John Fortescue justly says, in any country or age, of which we know anything. He makes it a matter of reproach to the French, that they only eat bacon, and the heads and entrails of oxen and sheep, and that whilst their masters get the pullets, the eggs only are left for them; thus making a hardship of a diet of "eggs and bacon." This famous book was probably written about the year 1460—certainly not later. From this period up to the battle of Bosworth Field, and the accession of Henry the Seventh, is exactly a period of twenty-five years; during which the kingdom was at peace at home and abroad until the Earl of Richmond's enterprise, which after one battle made him king. A quarter of a century of quiet and security must have tended to increase the wealth and luxury which Fortescue so graphically describes; and yet, at this very time, we find a general alarm of the decay of population and the ruin of towns pervading the Statue Book, and continuing for a century and a half, until the seizure of the possessions of the Church first caused beggary and pauperism in England.

After Chief Justice Fortescue, the most valuable testimony as to the state of society in remoter times, is, perhaps, to be found in Fleetwood's "Chronicon Preciosum," or History of Prices from the earliest known records. Fleetwood's statements were probably in a great measure compiled from Acts of Parliament, County Rolls and Records, and other similar archives. Be that as it may, his statements, both as to wages and the prices of food and clothing, are generally borne out by the statutes passed by Parliament from time to time to regulate both the wages and dress of labouring persons; and the perusal of the whole must impress the most careless reader with a strong conviction of the ease and plenty which must have been felt throughout all society in these ages. The following table, which is compiled mostly from Fleetwood, but partly from the Statutes, gives a comparative view of the rules of wages and prices of necessaries from A.D. 1400 to A.D. 1650. The whole indicates a highly prosperous state, extending throughout all classes of society.

TABLE OF PRICES AND WAGES.

A.D. 1400.	s.	d.
Wheat, per quarter . .	8	0
Barley, ditto . . .	5	4
Fat sheep . . .	1	0
Ditto	0	10½
An ox carcass . .	7	6
A goose . . .	0	4
A lamb . . .	0	8
Best beer, per gallon .	0	1½
Claret ditto .	0	8

A.D. 1400.	s.	d.
Threshing grain, per qr. .	0	2½
A master mason's wages, per } day . . .	0	4
Making 100 faggots .	0	7
Reaping grain, per acre .	0	9
Sawing per 100 ft. of deal	1	1
A labourer's wages, per day	0	3

1450.	s.	d.
Wheat (plentiful), per quarter	5	4
Finest ditto ditto .	8	0
Oats ditto .	2	1
A lean ox . .	13	0
A veal or calf . .	2	0
A goose . . .	0	3
A lamb . . .	1	0
Eggs, per hundred .	0	5
Red wine, per gallon .	1	0

1450.	s.	d.
A tiler and man, per day .	1	2
A mower, with diet, ditto	0	4
A reaper, with diet, ditto .	0	3
A tiler, ditto . . .	0	6
A man and cart, ditto .	1	8
A master carpenter, ditto .	0	10
A sawyer, ditto .	0	6
A labourer, per three days	1	4
A weeder, per day . .	0	2

1454.	s.	d.
Malt (plenty), per quarter .	2	8
Ditto ditto .	1	4
An ox . . .	12	0
Ale, per gallon .	0	1

1480.	s.	d.
Wheat, per quarter . .	4	4
Oats, ditto . . .	2	0

1500.	s.	d.
Wheat, per quarter . .	7	4
Malt, ditto . .	2	8
A cow . . .	8	0
A lamb . . .	1	0
A pig . . .	0	5
Eggs, per hundred .	0	9
Wine, per gallon .	1	0
Ditto, ditto .	0	8
Carcass of a neat .	0	10

1500.	s.	d.
A carpenter, with diet, per } day . . .	0	6
A plumber, ditto, ditto .	0	6
A tiler or joiner, ditto .	0	6
Lesser crafts, without diet, } per day . . .	0	6
A mower, ditto, ditto .	0	4
A reaper, ditto, ditto .	0	3
A carter, ditto, ditto .	0	3
A woman labourer, ditto .	0	2½

1550.

	£	s.	d.
Wheat, per quarter .	0	14	8
Ditto (scarcity), ditto	1	0	0
Barley ditto	0	5	0
A steer, fat . .	1	5	0
Mutton, per carcass .	0	5	8
A wedder . .	0	4	4

1550.

	s.	d.
A mower's *statute* wages, with diet, per day }	0	4
A mower, without diet, do.	0	10
A binder and shearer, with diet, per day }	0	2
A shearer, without diet, do.	0	5
A journeyman tailor, with diet, ditto . . }	0	4

1570.

Wheat (scarcity), per qr.	0	16	0

1570.

Labourers, without diet, per day . . . }	0	5

1575.

Wheat, per qr. .	1	0	0

1585.

Wheat (scarcity), per qr.	1	4	0
A calf or veal . .	0	7	4
Barley, per quarter .	0	13	0

1600.

Wheat, per quarter .	1	1	0
Barley, ditto . .	0	13	0
A sheep . . .	0	6	4
A goose . . .	0	1	0
Six pigeons . .	0	0	6

1600.

A labourer, per day . .	0	10

1610 to 1650.

A fat ox . . .	9	10	0
Mutton, per of stone 8lb.	0	2	3
A veal . . .	0	17	0
A lamb . . .	0	6	8
Tongues, cured, per doz.	0	12	0
A chine of beef .	0	18	0
Wheat, per quarter .	1	14	0
Ditto, ditto . .	2	0	0

1610 to 1650.

A master mason, per day .	1	6
A mason, with diet, ditto .	1	0
Apprentice masons, ditto .	0	10
Apprentices, with diet, do.	0	4
Millwrights, ditto . .	1	6
Plough-wrights, ditto .	1	6
Labourers, ordinary, ditto	0	10
Journeymen artizans, ditto	1	2
Reapers, ditto .	1	4
Women shearers, ditto .	1	2
Plumbers, ditto .	1	4
Glaziers, ditto .	1	4
Collar-makers, ditto .	1	6
Armourers, ditto .	1	6
Knackers, ditto .	1	6

In reading the above table, it must always be remembered that the wages quoted by Fleetwood were regulated for the most part by statute, and not by supply and demand. The labourers, being few comparatively, would not bind themselves to work, excepting for ample wages; and this disposition to force exorbitant wages, as it was called, on the part of the labouring people, was attempted to be put down by statutes, which professed to regulate the rates of hire to be paid to different handicrafts. As trade increased, however, it was found that this maximum could not be enforced in the walled towns, and especially at the sea-ports, where there was a growing demand for labourers. Hence there was a constant struggle on the part of the young husbandmen to get to the sea-ports. They crossed the country in bands of a dozen together, carrying quarter-staffs, begging their way, and threatening those who would not give alms; and hence arose the terms " sturdy beggar" and " staff-striker" in the old statutes. To stop this, Acts were passed to forbid husbandmen entering walled towns: they were all, however, evaded, and the foolish attempt forcibly to regulate wages was gradually abandoned. All this, however, goes to prove the great comfort with which at this period the common people unquestionably lived. We see an artizan earning in three or four days as much as would buy a sheep, a calf, or a quarter of barley or malt. We see wine and beer the common drink of the people; and when we come to examine the statutes relative to food and apparel, we shall find that butchers' meat was the ordinary food of all, and that their dress was of the best and costliest description. To these statutes let us now turn.

The Acts, in which the sort of food upon which the English people lived is most distinctly described, are those which were passed during the reign of Henry the Eighth, against monopolies of grazing stock and the consolidation of grazing farms; the mention being incidental, and by the way, adds to the value of the evidence, the facts being alluded to as being well known, and indeed perfectly notorious. The cause of the Acts was the great and steady rise in the prices of all sorts of commodities, which took place during this reign, and has gone on down to our own time. The cause of this rise was the discovery of the gold and silver mines of Mexico and Peru, and the constant addition to the quantity of money in circulation that was,

as a consequence, going on. At the time, however, this was not understood. The rise of
prices, instead of being attributed to the depreciation of the value of money, and its increased
quantity, was held to be caused by monopoly,
and "forestalling and regrating," as it was
termed, and hence Acts were passed to prevent
graziers accumulating enormous stocks of cattle
and sheep, or holding more than a limited number of acres of grass land. The Acts themselves
were futile, but the testimony as to the quality
of the food of the people, which they inciden-
tally embody, is invaluable. Thus the statute
passed in the twenty-fifth year of Henry the
Eighth, chap. xiii., has for its object to limit
the number of cattle and sheep held by any
individual; but in the preamble, it complains
that such has been the rise in the prices of
" corn, cattell, wooll, pigs, geese, hens, chickens,
and egges," the ordinary articles "in use by all
subjects," that (says the Act) "many have not
been able to buy them." In like manner, the
Act passed in the twenty-fourth year of the same
reign, chap, iii., declares " beef, mutton, pork,
and veal" to be the food in ordinary " of the
poorer sort." Thus, then, it is past a doubt
that, throughout the whole period referred to by

Sir Frederick Morton Eden, animal food was the common and daily fare of the people ; and when, in addition to the evidence of Chief Justice Fortescue, we look at the laws for regulating the prices of the cloth to be worn by labouring men, we are forced upon the conclusion that, whilst the population was going back, an abundance, bordering on luxury, was reigning and prevalent throughout England. It may be proper to remark also, that both fruit and vegetables, and, to a certain extent, grain, seem to have been, up to a late period, neglected, and hardly to have constituted an article of diet. Butchers' meat, with a little bread, and poultry and eggs, was their food. On fast days, fish must have been the resource ; as it is well known that most of the fruit and vegetables now in use were of comparatively modern introduction. The English seem to have left it to the Dutch to cultivate the arts of gardening aud planting ; and Holland was the great mart both for trees, garden vegetables, and flowers, down to a late period of English history.

The strong testimony of Fortescue as to the costly apparel worn in his time by the English universally, has been already quoted. It is, however, abundantly corroborated by the Statute

Book, if corroboration were necessary. From
the reign of Edward the Third, to that of
Elizabeth, not less than ten distinct statutes for
regulating the apparel of servants and labourers
were passed! To all these it would be unneces-
sary to recur, but a recapitulation of the objects
of some of them is both instructive and curious.
In the third year of Edward III., chapter iv.,
is an Act against luxury in apparel. It limits
the wearing of furs to persons of a certain rank,
and in certain offices. In the thirty-seventh year
of the same king's reign, was passed another
long Act, of many distinct sections or chapters,
regulating dress from that of the gentleman
down to that of the day-labourer. In year iii.
of Edward the Fourth, chapter v., a similar
statute was enacted, and in the fifth year of the
same reign, chapter xiii., another statute to
prohibit gilding, and wearing gold and silver lace,
except by certain ranks, and this at a period
when gold and silver were twenty times their
present value! That this wonderful amount of
wealth and comfort, distributed throughout an
entire people, had been of long growth, seems
not to be doubtful. The truth seems to be,
that the Norman Invaders and their power—
like the Tartars, and other Tribes, that from time

to time overran and subdued China—were swallowed up and submerged amidst the greater numbers of the people whom they nominally ruled. Feudalism was, after the lapse of two centuries, only a name, and real independence and wealth seem to have grown, during the lapse of a few reigns, to a height hardly to be surpassed. As early as the period A.D. 1300 complaints of the luxury of the people begin to appear both in the Chronicles and Histories of the time, and in the Statute Book; and as the best proof of the actual wealth and comfort of the people, may be cited the provisions of an Act of Parliament, passed in 1363, that is to say, towards the end of the splendid and prosperous reign of Edward the Third, the greatest of the extraordinary family of the Plantagenets. In this Act, tradesmen and artificers, being mastermen, are allowed to wear fine woollen cloth, as high as *one shilling and sixpence the yard*. Ploughmen, hinds, pig-drivers, and others are limited not to wear cloth of a greater price than *one shilling* the yard. Now, as in the reign of Edward the Third, it is certain that money was of nearly twenty times its present value, this is equivalent to prohibiting tradesmen and artizans from wearing cloth, if at or about the price of *thirty shillings the yard*, and labourers from wearing it if it cost more than *eighteen or twenty shillings the yard*—a prohibition at which both tradesmen and labouring men of the present day would stare!

Upon a review of all these facts, the conclusion seems to be undeniable, that a decay or diminution of the population was an observable and admitted fact, from about A.D. 1480, until the expiration of about a century and a half after that time ; that both prior to, and during the whole period, ease, comfort, and plenty were predominant in England ; that the food of the people was chiefly animal food ; and that beer, ale, and wine were so plentiful that every man brewed his own beer, and such was the use of French wines, that, according to Froissart, in the reign of Edward III., " a fleet of more than " two hundred English merchantmen was seen " at the single port of Bourdeaux, to import wine " alone :" that fine woollen stuffs, as well as gold and silver lace, and embroidery, were not uncommonly worn ; in short, that the Statutes against luxury went hand in hand with those complaining of the decay of towns, and decrease of the people! And what is still more remarkable, this decay of towns, villages, and mansions of all sorts, throughout the country, was going on at the very period when architecture, both ecclesiastical and civil, had attained in England—as witness the noble chapel of Henry the Seventh—the highest pitch of gorgeous magnificence to which it ever rose in these Islands, and from which it was fated speedily, that is to say, in the coursé of another century, to decline, perhaps, for ever.

That this extraordinary state of things is easily explicable upon the theory of population now attempted to be established, is sufficiently apparent ; but the author submits that it must remain a difficulty insuperable under any other hitherto brought before the world.

The gross and plentiful diet of the period above refered to, as compared with the present mode of living in England, by all ranks, is certainly a curious subject for contemplation. Up to the end of Elizabeth's reign, tea and coffee seem to have been totally unknown even to the households of the Nobility, and sugar an article of great luxury. In the household book of Philip, the third Lord Wharton, of which the entries for one year are preserved in the Archæologia Æliana, vol. ii., commencing

with October in the twenty-seventh year of the
reign of Elizabeth, neither tea nor coffee are
ever mentioned. Sugar, in small quantities,
at an enormous price, appears classed amongst
the spicery, but so dear that a pound is set
down as costing eighteen and nineteen-pence—
about half the price of the carcass of a sheep,
or mutton, as given in the same page, which
are rated at three shillings and threepence per
sheep, whether with or without the skin does
not appear. In point of fact, animal food,
with wine or beer, seems to have been the food
of the whole people, and eaten at all meals and
all times of day—saving on fast days, when
fish was used. In Lord Wharton's household
book oatmeal is only twice mentioned. The
warm drinks, called possets and hot tankards,
were spiced compositions of wine or ale, eggs,
and seasonings ; and the gruels and frumeties
were similarly enriched. Fish seems to have
brought very high prices ; and a porpoise, under
the title of a " porpus pigge," is rated at *two
shillings*, and a " salte salmon" at the same
rate, an immense price in these days. Poultry
and wild-fowl seem also to have sold high, as
compared with ordinary meat, a hen being set

down at fourpence, or six shillings for eighteen.
In short, it is clear that beef, mutton, veal, and
pork were the chief and ordinary food of the
people, with bread and ale, or wine, or sometimes
cider.   Culinary vegetables and fruits seem to
have been totally neglected; so much was this
the case, that Katharine of Aragon, when queen,
sent to Flanders for a salad ; and carrots,
turnips, parsnips, and celery were imported from
Holland ! To show how cheap solid living was,
and how easily the rates of wages given enabled
the people to procure it, it may be worth while
to quote the allowance made to the Lady Anne,
daughter of King Edward the Third, married to
Lord Howard, son of the Earl of Surrey.   To
keep herself, one gentlewoman, one woman, one
girl, one gentleman, one yeoman, and three
grooms, she was allowed one pound eleven
shillings per week, this including clothing,
wages, &c. ! For the support of seven horses,
horse furniture, &c., the allowance was twenty-
five pounds ten shillings and fourpence per
annum ! This was a princess's allowance, and
occurred probably about fifty years before Chief
Justice Fortescue wrote his book describing the
state of England.   In twenty-five years after

that, in the midst of all this plenty, the decay of population and towns is the subject of national alarm!

One other truth we learn from the foregoing considerations, and that is, how absurd the idea is, that increase of buildings is necessarily a sure sign of prosperity in a district. It is clear it is often the contrary. As the poorer part of the population becomes more dense, the old buildings are let into small tenements, and it becomes necessary to build other houses for the more wealthy—a consequence not of increased prosperity, but of an increased poor and needy population.

Leaving now the history of his own country, in times comparatively modern, the author would direct the reader's attention to the annals of a time much more remote, that is to say, to the earlier period of the decline of the Roman Empire. When we look at the great cause of this decline from its beginning to its end, we see an Empire of enormous power and amazing extent gradually brought to the ground by a long succession of attacks by unknown foreign barbarian tribes, whose course may be described in general terms as tending from the north-east to the south-west. As these attacking tribes

succeeded each other, they brought with them
different names, and different and most vague
accounts of their origin and original country.
The Cimbri, the Teutones, and Ambrones, were
considered to belong to Germany, and in all
likelihood properly so considered. Yet it seems
to be probable that the battles of the Consul
Marius with these tribes, were only some of the
first symptoms of a gradual movement south-
westward, passing through Germany and France
towards Italy, and precursors of those various
incursions which continued by various tribes,
under the names of Goths, Visigoths, Ostrogoths,
Vandals, Huns, and the more polished and
familiar name of Persians, Ottomans, Moors,
and Saracens, at last brought the empire of the
Cæsars to the dust, and broke up the very form
and image into which Roman greatness had
moulded Europe, and much of Asia and Africa.
On a calm review of this mighty movement, it
seems difficult, almost impossible, to believe that
a continuity of action, spreading over so many
centuries, should have its origin in the mere
capricious ambition of many various tribes accidentally taking one general direction; or that, in
fact, it originated, properly speaking, in ambition
or caprice at all. The love of country and locality

is universal. Ambition leads nations to extend their empires, and increase their power and name, but not to leave their seats and migrate to other climates. Caprice never did this, neither did ambition, though both have done strange things. On the contrary, the more we look at the course of the world, as it is known since the latter times of the Roman Commonwealth, down to the extinction of the empire, the more we must feel convinced that some great and pervading cause must have been at the bottom, and constituted the source of this great south-western movement, of which, perhaps, the earliest European pulse may have been the first rush of the Gauls upon the young Republic of Rome, and the last, the sack of Constantinople by Mahomet the Second. The first great stride of this movement was made by the Goths. Of their origin all the accounts are involved in obscurity. Gibbon, upon the authority of Jornandes and others, seems inclined to give some credit to their own almost unintelligible traditions, which assigned to their native country the Ancient Scandinavia, or the region which is now known as Sweden. This strange account is, however, highly improbable on the face of it; and how a remote country north of the Baltic, to this hour thinly peopled, should

send forth to overrun Poland and Prussia and the
countries bordering on the Danube, a multitude
sufficient to alarm the Roman armies stationed
in Dacia, and looking on the Danube as a great
boundary, those who believe it may describe or
account. Upon a calmer view it seems more
rational to esteem the tribes known as Goths,
Visigoths, Ostrogoths, and Vandals, as the advanced guard of that innumerable and unknown
horde of nations living in the more northern
parts of Asia and the eastern parts of Europe,
which, by causes to be explained, were gradually
driven westward, and precipitated, in the lapse of
centuries, one after the other upon the boundaries
of the Roman Empire. That this is the almost
certain truth, is evident in what is known of the
history of their successors in spoliation and conquest, the Huns. These barbarians, from their features as described by all the historians, were clearly
Calmucks ; the small eyes, the strange features,
and the different bodily formation, clearly refer
them to the regions now known as the borders of
China and Hindostan. Gibbon places their
country to the north of the Chinese wall, and it
is evidently his opinion, that it was not until a
long series of conflicts with the enormous and
growing multitudes inhabiting what is now termed

China Proper, that they turned their arms westward, and following the course of the Goths
towards Germany, at last pushed, by their *mo-
mentum*, their predecessors the Goths over the
Danube, upon the Dacian provinces of Rome,
in the reign of the weak Emperor Valens, who
consented to the passage of his now suppliant
barbarian enemies.

Still the cause of the continued human pressure
westward, through so many centuries, seems
altogether mysterious and inexplicable upon the
ordinary motives that actuate masses of people.
To read the latter portion of Roman history as
it stands, gives the idea of large masses of
barbarians from the north-east being smitten,
like the animal called the "lemming," with an
indescribable love of movement in a certain
direction, and precipitating themselves, in spite
of slaughter and defeat, by millions after millions
upon the western world.   For all this there must
have existed some great continuous and pervading cause ; and this cause is probably to be
sought and found in the state and condition
of the races of people inhabiting those vast
and now thickly-peopled regions, known in
modern times as China, Ava, Cochin China,
Chinese Tartary, Hindostan, Delhi, and the

countries west of the Indus, including Affgha-
nistan, Caubul, Lahore, and the Punjaub, until
we come to the frontiers of Persia, and the hilly
countries lying towards the Caspian and Euxine.

If there is any remote historical truth established by a mass of evidence that may be called
undeniable, it is that the countries above
enumerated have been in the state of semi-
civilization, in which they now are for a very
long, though probably, undefinable period.
Without giving much of implicit or unlimited
credence to their own chronicles, traditions, and
annals, it is yet evident that their state of society
bears the general impress of age. Everything
we can see and learn tends to establish this.
The disposition of the people themselves, their
singularly great, though to us imperfect progress
in literature and the arts; their histories, their
religion, and their monuments, all irresistibly
lead to this conclusion; and it appears to be
impossible not to believe that the state of society
which at present exists amidst the hundreds of
millions which swarm over the districts of China
and Hindostan, has not so existed, or nearly so,
for very many centuries; and that of most of the
arts of life they possess a knowledge long
anterior to that of even the oldest countries of

Europe. Hence we are compelled to think that the modes of life and manners which to this hour are in full force over these thickly-peopled regions, must have been of ancient and slow formation; and though we may not, with the Chinese, date their empire beyond the time fixed by Christians for the creation of the world, we can hardly deny, that, as a people, they are probably the most ancient existing. Here then we see, growing gradually through many and very distant centuries, a system of society which has been proved by the facts to have been so wonderfully favourable to the growth of an enormous and dense population, that, in the regions enumerated, though their area is but a small fragment of the habitable globe, are probably congregated a full fourth part of all mankind. Nay, perhaps, the third part would be the more judicious position, if the estimated numbers of mankind are not held to exceed two thousand millions of persons. For, taking the population of the Chinese Empire at about three hundred millions, which is generally believed to be the fact; Japan, Cochin China, the Burman Empire, Correa, and the other dependencies of China at seventy millions; the peninsula of Hindostan, from the Indus to the Ganges, at one hundred and sixty millions ; and making allowance for the numerous population that lies between the Indus westward, and the Frontiers of Persia, we attain to a multitude of beings hardly to be conceived, though not difficult to be numbered, and probably amounting to nearly one-third part of all the human beings now living upon this globe. Now, in the growth and extension of this enormous population over the regions which they inhabit, but in which they are still as it were cooped up—for a population so dense exists in no other parts of the known world—we see the continuous cause of the gradual and progressive migration of all the more scattered tribes which this vast population must have gradually displaced. That the extension of the vast population of China went on amidst perpetual wars with the Calmuck tribes, who were their neighbours, we have light enough from history to show. The same light, however, discovers to us the very natural fact, that the conquerors of China were eventually swallowed up in the enormous multitudes of the conquered ; and that hence hostilities were useless as any permanent check to the extension of these myriads throughout such climates as permitted the continuation of their peculiar mode of life. Hence the Huns, after overrunning China again and again, were at last pushed westward upon the Goths, whom they, in their turn, precipitated upon the Roman Empire in the first instance, and then followed. In fact, climate was the only stay to the extension of a people, who had neither animal food, nor the olive, nor the vine; and it was not until China and India extended their dense hordes to colder and more hilly climates—to Tartary, to Thibet, to Nepaul, and towards the Indian Caucasus—that their numbers began to thin, and the limit that we now see as bounding their empire, was established. What the Huns and Tartars could not do, climate has effected. As soon as the pastoral life was forced upon them, and rice was no longer the staple of subsistence, their numbers ceased to grow, and extended boundaries became no longer a matter of paramount and physical necessity, uncontrollable by the surrounding nations. In the long process of the growth of this immense eastern population we obtain a clue to the cause which must through many centuries have disturbed, and driven from their seats, the tribes that last, forced westward, trod down and eventually subverted the Roman Empire. How long the enormous populations of China and Hin-

dostan were in attaining their present extraordinary extent, it is impossible to say ; their
conflicts with the different Calmuck tribes must
no doubt have lengthened the term ; but in the
growth of these rice-fed millions we have an
explanation of historical phenomena, which seem
otherwise to be inexplicable, and which have
hitherto puzzled all inquirers.

Upon the whole, the author flatters himself
that the solution of the two historical difficulties
in question, which is afforded by this theory, are
strong collateral proofs of the soundness of the
theory itself. They are insoluble upon any other
hypothesis that has come under the author's
notice, and are of too striking and singular a
nature not to have perplexed most readers of
history.

CHAPTER VIII.

ARGUMENT FROM THE REVENUE.

—————

IF it were true that population has a natural
tendency to increase equally amongst all classes,
unchecked by anything but the inability to procure subsistence, the diseases which arise out of
a deficiency of nutriment, and the abandonment
of marriage caused by poverty and the fear of
it ; if this were true, then this is only affirming,
in another form of words, that the decrease of
a people must take place at the bottom of society,
and not in the middle or at the top ; for amongst
the higher or middle classes there can be neither
a want of subsistence, nor such a stringent fear
of poverty as to produce general celibacy. From
this it should seem of necessity to follow, that,
as a people increase in numbers, that increase
being from the richer, and not the poorest classes

of society, the power to contribute taxes must of course go on in nearly the same ratio with that of the increase of the numbers of the people. At all events it follows, upon this supposition, that one must increase with the other. This conclusion seems unavoidable when it is considered, that though the heads of a family may not make their children as rich as themselves, yet it cannot be supposed that their offspring do not contribute more or less to the taxes of the state. It is impossible to conceive this to be the case in a country like England, where almost all articles of ordinary consumption even are taxed, and where no man can escape indirect taxation, live as he may, not even the miserable Irish serf who exists upon potatoes; in short, if the population of England has increased in all classes, it seems impossible to doubt that taxation must have grown with the power of paying it, inasmuch as the consumption of tea, coffee, spirits, soap, tobacco, wine, and beer must, as a matter of course, have in a greater or less degree followed such an increase. The increased and added numbers amongst the higher and middling ranks must have derived from their parents, in the shape of saved capital, credit, and education, the ability to consume a share of taxed articles;

and therefore this sort of increase, if it really took place in a country, must be followed by an increase of ability to pay taxes, arising out of the added numbers to the wealthier classes. If, on the contrary, a population be increased by addition from the poorer classes alone, then it is evident that this addition may not be followed by any increased power of paying taxes, because the wages of labour may fall in such a proportion that the power to consume taxed articles may not be increased.

If, therefore, in any country the productiveness of the revenue is found to be at a standstill, whilst the numbers of the people are increased, it seems inevitably to follow, as a conclusion, that the increase must be altogether amongst the poor; for had it been equally diffused, the power of consuming taxed articles must in some degree, whether more or less, have been also increased, at all events for a time. The reader need hardly be told that this sort of proof, as how and whence population grows and increases, cannot be very visible save and except in countries very highly taxed, because it is the extreme of poverty only that can debar any portion of a people from using some of the comforts and luxuries of life. That the state of the revenue

of Great Britain, however, at this moment affords
this particular description of proof, the author is
well convinced; and it now remains to be shown
that such is the case.

If there is to be any faith placed in the returns
of the numbers of the population which have
from time to time been published and put forth
under the sanction of Government, the population in the year 1811 were twelve millions five
hundred and ninety-six thousand, eight hundred
and three persons. In 1839 they are estimated
at eighteen millions five hundred and twenty-four
thousand and thirty-six persons, with a probable
increase since that time. Such are asserted to
be the numbers of the population of Great Britain
at these two periods: what was the amount of taxation at each period? In 1811 the gross amount
of taxation was sixty-six millions, three hundred
and sixty-five thousand, five hundred and thirty-
five pounds. In 1839 the gross amount is only
fifty-four millions, one hundred thousand four
hundred and nine pounds, and of this last sum
a small portion is Irish taxes, the exchequers
being now blended; and yet it is notorious that
even this lesser amount in money cannot be continued to be paid by the increased millions of
population, as in spite of an addition of five per

cent. added to the taxes in 1840, the revenue has absolutely decreased and not increased. The author is not unaware that as it stands, and upon the face of it, this is an unfair statement and a false comparison, because unquestionably the value of money in the year first named, 1811, was less than in 1839 and 1840. But even deducting one-third, or thirty-three per cent. for depreciation, the value of the taxes in 1811 still stands at forty-four millions. If, then, twelve millions of people could pay in 1811 forty-four millions of pounds in taxes, eighteen millions ought, if the increase was diffused equally over all classes, to be able to pay, with the same ease, sixty-six millions ; but it is proved that they cannot, with Ireland aiding, pay fifty-four millions ; therefore the increase has been chiefly amongst the poor, or this could not have happened: *q. e. d.*

In stating this result, it ought not to be forgotten that the poor's-rate has been forcibly depressed below the level at which it stood in 1811, by a severe and stringent law ; and yet the saving arising from this operation of the New Poor Law has not caused an ability to pay taxes at all commensurate with that of 1811, which adds greatly to the force of the reasoning already adduced, and to the high probability of the truth of the conclusion to which it leads. The great increase of poor-rates which had in 1833-4, notwithstanding the difference in value of money caused by the Currency Bill of 1819, touched nearly the highest amount at the end of the war in 1815, and which caused " the Poor Law Amendment Bill," is also a strong corroborative testimony of the same truth—that increase of population is ever amongst the poor ; and that, *as* is the poverty of living, *so* is the tendency to multiply.

CHAPTER IX.

ARGUMENT FROM THE RECENT DECREASE OF THE
QUANTITY OF ANIMAL FOOD CONSUMED IN ENG-
LAND.

ALTHOUGH in preceding portions of this essay
the mode of living in the earlier times of England
has been described, and proved to be a diet of
beef, mutton, veal, and pork or bacon, it is not
inexpedient to show that a great alteration for
the worse in that diet is at this moment going
on in this country, where an increase of the
population is yearly taking place to a greater or
less extent. We have seen that, when butchers'
meat was the grand staple of subsistence the
numbers of the people tended to diminish. We
shall now see, that whilst the number of inhabitants are swelling yearly, their use of butchers'
meat is receding; that wine is drank only by
the rich; that even malt-liquor is comparatively

scarce; and that the consumption of potatoes has grown rapidly in modern times.

To show the actual diminution of the use of animal food throughout England is no easy matter. There are no returns in existence, probably, which would give the slaughter of cattle annually throughout the country at large; and those for London exhibit a false result, from the increased numbers of people daily, by the operation of artificial causes, located permanently or temporarily in the metropolis. Steam is increasing the number of visitants by thousands, and their increase, of course, causes an increase of permanent inhabitants; for inns, taverns, lodging-houses, &c., must be found for these erratic tribes, according to their demand for increased accommodation. Still there is a means of approximating to the facts, generally speaking, as to the national increase or decrease of animal diet. The calculation was made by the author of this treatise in the course of two letters to Lord Althorp, then Chancellor of the Exchequer, which were reprinted in ' Cobbett's Political Register," 13th of April and 25th of May, 1833. The object of the author was to show the increase of fraud in the Excise duties on soap; but in the course of his proof, it became necessary to show that the amount of tallow produced in England had greatly decreased, and a decrease of tallow is a decrease of butchers' meat. The mode taken was as follows, and the result, the author has reason to believe, is near the truth.

Two years were taken between which to institute a comparison; and on account of some of the documents for these years being more perfect than those of other years, the periods of 1815 and 1829 were selected. The process of calculation is as follows. It was computed by those most conversant in the tallow trade, that, in the year of 1815, the produce of tallow from cattle slaughtered in England was from 50,000 tons to 53,000 tons in all. This estimate was, however, of tallow in the rough state, before being melted and refined. To get the quantity of merchantable tallow, a fifth of the whole weight must be deducted as refuse; and therefore the quantity of available tallow produced in Great Britain in 1815 may be safely set down at forty-one thousand tons at least, and certainly at no less a quantity. Now then, it was known that in the year 1815 the tallow produced in England made all the candles manufactured in England, and left a *surplus.* This was a noto-

rious fact to all whose interest it was to know it.
Almost every chandler in England, after making
his year's candles, had a small *remanet* of tallow ;
and this he was in the habit of selling to the
soap-makers, who used it for making hard soap
along with imported foreign tallow from Russia
or Buenos Ayres. The tallow consumed in the
manufacture of candles of all sorts in 1815 was
thirty-eight thousand tons only, leaving, as the
surplus or *remanet*, the quantity required to
make up the forty-one thousand tons produced.
The population, at that period, may be safely
estimated at thirteen millions in round numbers
at the most. This was the state of things in
1815 as to this question. Let us now jump
to 1829, a period of fourteen years ; and sub-
jecting it to the same examination, note down
the results. The year 1829 was a year of considerable plenty, as far as the seasons, both for
tillage and grazing, were concerned ; and it was
also a year of comparatively low prices, for, in
the April of this year, all bank-notes under five
pounds were withdrawn from circulation, and
the depression of prices which naturally followed
this measure, happened accordingly. The consequence was, that the consumption of butchers'
meat was, in all probability, above that which

would have taken place under ordinary circumstances; and yet it was far from commensurate with the increase of the people, whose numbers had by this time reached the amount of sixteen millions of persons. Such was the population: the amount of home-produced tallow was great, though not great in proportion, and reached, by the best calculations, nearly as far as forty-seven thousand tons of good, merchantable, available tallow, being an increase of six thousand tons upon the produce of 1815. The demand for candles had, however, after the end of the war, increased in a greater ratio. The manu-factories had, owing to the throwing open of the continental field, been enormously multiplied. The night was made to supply its relays of workmen as well as day; and hence, though gas was now beginning to be generally used, and also oil lamps of superior manufacture, the necessity for candles had rather outstripped the growth of the people, and the amount of tallow made into candles in 1829 is very large, amounting, as it did in that year, to fifty-two thousand tons of tallow. Thus, then, with an increased demand for labour, but also with an increased population, the result is, that in 1829 the tallow produced in this country was so far from making all the candles wanted, and leaving a surplus, that it was actually deficient by the amount of five thousand tons of tallow. This statement admits of being verified to some extent, and this verification was exhibited as follows.

It has been stated that the surplus home-produced tallow, after the making of all the candles in the kingdom, was sold by the tallow-chandlers and candle-makers to the manufacturers of hard soap. This was the case up to the end of the war in 1815; but after that time the case was gradually reversed, and the makers of tallow candles, instead of having an annual surplus to sell, became, after a few years, buyers of foreign tallow to supply the deficiency, which now began to be felt, of the produce at home This foreign tallow was, throughout the country, naturally supplied to the candle-makers by the soap-makers, who were always, of necessity, holders of foreign tallow, and who, being dispersed throughout all the large towns, were at hand to supply it.

Here then was a *datum* or *calculus* supplied. The makers of soap cultivated this tallow trade in proportion to their means and capital; and if, therefore, it was ascertained what proportion

of the soap of the kingdom was made in any one
large town, the amount of tallow supplied by the
soap-makers to the tallow-chandlers might safely
be calculated to be in the same *ratio*, as to the
trade in tallow of this sort throughout the
country. This calculation was accordingly gone
into, and the town of Newcastle-upon-Tyne
taken as the criterion. In the year 1829, the
hard soap made in Newcastle-upon-Tyne was
one-fourteenth of the whole known to be made in
the kingdom of Great Britain. The number of
casks of tallow supplied by the soap-makers to
the tallow-chandlers was then accurately ascertained ; and they amounted to within a trifle of
nine hundred casks of Russian yellow candle
tallow. Nine hundred casks multiplied by
fourteen gives twelve thousand six hundred
casks ; these twelve thousand six hundred casks
would as nearly as possible amount to *five thousand* tons of tallow ; and this, curiously enough,
agrees exactly with the difference between the
weight of candles made, and the home produce
of tallow in 1829. It is probable that the
greater strictness as to the collection of the
Revenue in 1829 would increase the amount of
candles made, more than the tenth as compared
with the returns of 1815 ; still, however, it

cannot be doubted that the calculations on the whole approximate tolerably closely to the actual truth.

Thus, then, it appears that, if to the excess of three thousand tons, in 1815, be added the deficiency of five thousand tons of tallow, produced at home in 1829, the whole falling off is eight thousand tons of tallow. The proportion that tallow bears to lean in cattle is averaged as *one* to *ten*. Here then we have proof of a diminution in one year, 1829, of *eighty thousand tons* in the consumption of beef alone ; which, at the rate of half a pound per day for the individual, would be a fair supply for a million of persons, or two hundred thousand families. If to this we add the diminution to a corresponding extent in the consumption of mutton, the tallow of which does not, in any great degree, enter into the composition of tallow candles, and some diminution even in the use of bacon, we cannot but doubt that the addition of three millions of persons to the population, during the fourteen years intervening between 1815 and 1829, was made in company with a vast decrease in the consumption of animal food ; and that, therefore, the probability is, that the increase of people was nearly altogether amongst the poor. That this was certainly the case, there is, however, other corroborating evidence.

First, we have the rapid increase of the poor's-rates, which, ever since the population was known to be decisively upon the increase, have gone on, in spite of all the efforts of Ministers and Parliaments to narrow the amount of relief, with redoubled strides, and since the accession of George the Third, in 1760, when their amount was under two millions annually, have more than tripled themselves! Again, we have the decreased consumption of malt, which, before the passing of the first Act to impose a tax on it, in the year 1662, was used by the people, it is believed, to three times its present extent. Since then the population has gone on growing, and the consumption of the nutritious beverage of malt liquor has gone on diminishing. Even up to the middle of the last century, and later than that, not only most of the persons inhabiting towns, but all the agricultural labourers, brewed their own beer. The knowledge of brewing all over England was as universal as is the knowledge of making bread all over the North of England at this hour. Every Northumberland, Cumberland, Durham, Yorkshire, Lancashire, and Westmoreland servant could not

only bake but brew ; and the same knowledge
of beer-making extended all over England.
Such now is the disuse of malt liquor, that this
general knowledge is now at an end, and confined to a trade.   If increased population, with
decreased means, goes on, the art of bread-making
will soon be similarly lost even in the North,
where the cheapness of fuel has hitherto preserved it.   In addition to this proof of decreased
solidity of subsistence having marched step by
step with the march of population, is the increased
cultivation and use of the potato as an article
of staple diet.   It is confidently stated in agricultural reports, and by practical farmers, that
the culture of the potato in England itself (leaving
out Ireland and Scotland) has quadrupled during
the last hundred years.   This is asserted as a
known and admitted fact in the *Mark Lane
Express* in 1837, and the *known* consumption
of potatoes in London alone, for the preceding
year, is affirmed to be as high as one hundred
and eighty-five thousand six hundred and fifty
tons weight !   A plain proof that great numbers
even of the metropolitan populace must subsist
almost entirely upon this miserable root ;   for, at
the rate of three pounds of potatoes per day, this
would subsist three hundred and fifty thousand

grown persons, which is equal to a full third of the population of the metropolis! The *known* consumption must, however, be under the *real* consumption ; and if this be true of luxurious London, what must be the case in other poorer parts of the country ? Such are the facts ; and yet, with these facts, we find, in companionship, the fact that English population is steadily upon the increase.

There is one other observation to be made, which, though it does not apply to England, is yet not out of place here. It is this, that almost the only spot on the inhabited globe where systematic cannibalism has been incontestibly proved to prevail, is all but destitute of animal or even nutritious vegetable food, and when first discovered was even more so than it is at this time. This place is New Zealand, which, until a colony was planted there by the English from Australia within the last twenty years, was in this condition. From what is now known, it seems clear that when first discovered by Tasman in 1642, these Islands were nearly destitute of any quadruped whatever, and that even of nutritive vegetables their produce was nearly *nil*. Of indigenous quadrupeds, there were a few of a species of wild dog or fox, some rats, a species

of bat, and perhaps the alligator ; but this is still
uncertain, and will probably, from the nature of
the streams, not turn out to be the case.   The
birds principally were wild pigeons, wild ducks,
and some parroquets and sea-gulls.   In fact, the
natives lived chiefly upon the root of a wild fern,
and upon fish, which are plentiful on the coasts,
until their numbers probably at last induced the
hideous practice of subsisting upon each other.
That constant wars were followed by feasts on
human flesh, until the custom of eating each
other at last became perfectly common and
habitual, is now ascertained.   This is ascribed
by some to superstition ; and superstition may
have been a cause or pretext, but it is probable
that sheer hunger had much to do with the
establishment of a taste so utterly revolting and
horrible.   It may be said that the numbers of
this people are not great in comparison with the
area of the islands.   This is true, but then it
must be remembered, they have been kept down
by perpetual slaughter, both on a large and small
scale ; that they have no great extent of land fit for
cultivation ; and that they were, until Cook visited
them, destitute of anything worth cultivation.   Of
the roots and seeds which he left, only the potato
and turnip are remaining ; and they are grown

in the rudest way only in scattered plots round
the coast. In fact, the interior of the whole land
is lofty Alpine mountains, washed by rapid
streams, with snowy summits at the greatest
elevations, and the lower valleys and ravines
covered with gigantic and inexhaustible timber;
but these regions are totally solitary and unin-
habited forests, growing little or nothing for the
food of man; in short, umbrageous deserts. The
way in which the natives lived is evident in their
few arts; they were expert in making lines of
wild flax, in catching fish, and in cooking them;
and an occasional whale or the seal were great
delicacies. They could also snare birds, but
their epicurism was in human flesh; the roasted
or baked thigh of a girl of fourteen or fifteen
being described by them as the greatest known
delicacy, and in terms according exactly with the
language of Swift's ironical " proposal for eating
the children of the poor in Ireland!" To the
author, it appears hardly possible to conceive that
so shocking a state of life and society could have
arisen from anything short of a surplus population
totally destitute of food. In the winter, which is
stormy in that latitude, vegetables must have been
scarce, and fish for a length of time often unattain-
able by a people who had not the art of curing them

for keeping. That upon such diet, their numbers would soon outstrip their powers of obtaining food, seems to the author sufficiently proved; and to a people so placed, with neither religion nor morality to plead against it, the palpable and necessary, and only resource, was cannibalism. The " Arreoys" of Otaheite were the step *next* to this.

Upon the whole, the author trusts he has made it abundantly apparent, that where a population rapidly increases, it will be found to do so always in company with poverty of living; that the increase will be amongst the poor, and will march at the exact pace of the advance of the hardship and meagreness of living amongst those who so increase.

CHAPTER X.

ARGUMENT FROM THE CURRENT OPINIONS OF MAN-
KIND IN PAST TIME.

IF mankind had been in a constant universal
and invariable state of increase from the beginning, save and except only when and where
such increase was violently stopped by starvation
or the intense dread of it—by slaughter, whether
of war or domestic—by pestilence, or by
elemental convulsion, this law could hardly
have failed to become apparent to mankind in
general. It is hardly possible to conceive of
such a state of natural arrangement, and at the
same time to conceive that this constant and
universal increase, or tendency to it, should have
remained undiscovered from one age to another;
and mankind to have lived under such a striking
natural dispensation as this, century after cen-

tury, for thousands of years, all the time blind to and unconscious of it. If, however, we look at the opinions of former times as to this momentous matter, as far as such can be collected from the writings that survive, we shall find the current of opinion setting generally in the contrary direction, and a constant recurrence of traditions amongst the old authors that the world, or particular districts of it, had been much more populous formerly than it was at the period when they wrote, or near to that period. The best " bird's-eye view" of the notions and traditions of the Greek and Roman writers as to the population of various countries at different periods is, perhaps, given by David Hume in his elaborate and learned essay " on the Populousness of Ancient Nations." In this essay he has collected, with much pains, the opinions of a great number of classic and other authors as to the state of population at various times and places ; and these opinions he examines after his usual acute method. Hume was at all times sufficiently disposed to be sceptical, but here he is perfectly excusable. Being himself destitute of any notion of the law which regulates population, and having apparently no theory, good, bad, or indifferent, as to the question, it is amusing to see how completely even his sagacious, cool, penetrating, and patiently inquiring mind is bewildered by the maze of evidence which, when brought together, the accounts of these writers may be properly styled. Hume's inclination is, as usual, to combat the generally received opinion. Many of the exaggerated statements as to numbers, of which the loose method of estimating multitudes, common to all times, but most common to ancient times, has been sufficiently prolific, he doubts, and successfully disproves. His grand puzzle, however, seems to lie in the various accounts of periods of *depopulation* which he adduces from different writers. These occur at the periods, and under the circumstances, when, if the theory now attempted to be established be founded in truth, they might be expected to occur, and of course to be placed by historians. The periods assigned, however, appear to Hume precisely those when no such phenomena ought to be expected; and after quoting and disbelieving various accounts of the decay of nations, he, at last, fairly confesses his complete bewilderment, and leaves this part of the question where he found it. In opposing what he deems exaggerated stories of population, and to explain the causes of periods of depopulation, which he is compelled to admit, he relies chiefly on the greater cruelty practised in former ages, the bloodiness of the battles, the massacre of prisoners, the harshness to slaves, and the devastations of conquerors; and the proneness of early annalists to the exaggeration of all accounts hinging upon considerations of number. Such are the general features of this celebrated and elaborate essay: let us now come to particulars.

In order to prove the prevalence of the opinion that in former times the numbers of mankind were greater than at subsequent periods, it is only requisite to quote the names of the principal authors whom Hume feels himself called upon to combat, in various ways, on the score of their statements as to the population of various nations and places, at various periods of time. Amongst the offenders in this way he enumerates Thucydides, Diodorus Siculus, Strabo, Herodotus, Plato, Theocritus, Polybius, Appian, Herodian, Athenæus, Demetrius Phalareus, Justin, Dionysius Halicarnassæus, Pliny the Elder, Plutarch, and Tacitus. Amongst the moderns he only mentions Vossius and Montesquieu; which last seems, from passages both in his "Persian Letters" and "Spirit of Laws" to have held stout opinions upon this subject. In his treatment of the exaggerated statements of these writers as to numbers, Hume is often ingenius, and sometimes in all human probability right. With their testimonies as to the decay and depopulation of different states at different periods, he finds it more difficult to deal. In fact, he is completely puzzled by them; and as the writers who give them do not attempt to explain them, they stand before the sceptical eye of Hume as a set of unaccountable anomalies and contradictions, incapable of explanation or of reconciliation with any known facts. Let us look at one or two of these passages.

ˋ " The laws, or as some writers call them, the " seditions of the Gracchi, were occasioned by " their observing the *increase* of slaves all over " Italy, and the *diminution* of free citizens. " Appian ascribes the increase to the propagation " of the slaves; Plutarch to the purchasing of " barbarians, who were chained and imprisoned " βαρβαρικα δεσμωτηρια. It is to be presumed " that both causes concurred."—*Essays,* vol. i. p. 387.

Here is an instance of *partial* depopulation in one class, with perhaps some increase in the other class, with which Hume is clearly puzzled. He does not attempt to explain it, and the explanations which he quotes are no explanations at all. The propagation of slaves to which Appian (Hist. Rom. lib. i.) refers, of course went on ; but what prevented the provincial free Roman citizens from propagating at the same rate ? Plutarch, in his "Lives of the Gracchi," attributes it to the purchase of more slaves. As their wealth increased this would probably be in accordance with the fact ; but to account for so marked a disproportion, and for that disproportion being used as an argument by Caius and Tiberius Gracchus for their " Agrarian laws," for *a new distribution of lands* amongst those who had served, was their object, we are compelled to admit a great and real diminution in the numbers of the Roman citizens, who held the provincial estates under the Republic. The facts, as stated by Appian and Plutarch, agree exactly with the statement made by Tacitus of the complete decay of the old Roman Patrician nobles in the time of Augustus; and upon the theory here insisted on, the whole is natural and probable in the highest degree. These men were the aristocracy of the provinces, and their decay only accords with the history of all aristocracies. Again—

" Polybius (Lib. ii.) says, that the Romans,

" between the first and second Punic Wars,
" being threatened with an invasion from the
" Gauls, mustered all their own forces and those
" of their allies, and found them to amount to
" seven hundred thousand men able to bear
" arms; a great number, surely, and which,
" when joined to the slaves, is probably *not less*,
" if not *rather more,* than that extent of coun-
" try affords at present. The enumeration, too,
" seems to have been made with some exactness;
" and Polybius gives us the detail of the parti-
" culars. But might not the number be magni-
" fied, in order to encourage the people? Dio-
" dorus Siculus makes the same enumeration
" amount to near a million. These variations
" are *suspicious.* He plainly, too, supposes that
" Italy in his time was *not* so populons; another
" *suspicious* circumstance. For who can believe
" that the inhabitants of that country *diminished*
" from the time of the first Punic War to that
" of the Triumvirate?"—*Essays*, vol. i., p. 413.

Of the foregoing passage, it may be with perfect fairness observed, that Mr. Hume's efforts
to throw suspicions on the statements of Polybius
and Diodorus, are not very happy. Polybius,
who was especially a writer of military knowledge, goes more into the *minutiæ* of the muster

than does Diodorus Siculus. After all, the difference is only between " more than seven hundred thousand " and a " million." As for the charge of exaggeration, it may be brought at any time, against anything, or anybody. Hume's especial bewilderment is apparent, however, in the concluding sentence. " Who can believe," he asks with astonishment, " that the population of that country diminished between the first Punic War and the Triumvirate ?" Now, if this theory of population which we are considering, be true, this is very easy to be believed. The Roman territory, at the time referred to by Diodorus and Polybius, was still narrow. The country that supplied these fighting men consisted, as Hume admits, of what now is the Pope's dominions, Tuscany, and a portion of the kingdom of Naples. At the time referred to, the inhabitants were the whole Roman people and their tributaries, and the population must accordingly have been of that miscellaneous sort which forms the average of a young nation, which has neither acquired great wealth nor great power. Of such a people the poor would be the majority; and if in the Republic there was then little wealth, we may be sure there was no luxury. Here are all the requisites for an increasing and somewhat dense population. If with this we compare the period of the Triumvirate, we shall find the very reverse state of things. Rome was then mistress almost of the known world. The wealth drawn into and about the city was enormous; and the whole regions alluded to belonged, past a doubt, to wealthy Roman citizens of all classes, from the patrician to the provincial free citizen. Here was a state of society precisely calculated to limit a population; want there could be none, generally speaking, and the chances are, there could hardly be a superfluous man in the whole district, save the household slaves of the landlords. Thus, then, narrowly looking at the statements of Polybius and Diodorus, and keeping in view the law of population now sought to be established, there seems every reason to believe them to be faithfully correct; and also that the belief of Diodorus Siculus that these districts were more populous then than in his time, is perfectly just, and in strict accordance with the probabilities deducible from known facts. The next passage is still more curious, from the bewilderment of all the writers as to the real causes of the decay or increase of a people.

" Were I (says Mr. Hume) to assign a period
" when I imagine this part of the world might
" possibly contain more inhabitants than at
" present, I should pitch upon the age of Trajan
" and the Antonines ; the great extent of the
" Roman empire being then civilised and culti-
" vated, settled almost in a profound peace, both
" foreign and domestic, and living under the
" same regular police and government. But we
" are told (by Montesquieu, l'Esprit de loix,
" 54, xxiii., cap. 19) that all *extensive* govern-
" ments, especially absolute monarchies, are
" *pernicious to population*, and contain a *secret*
" *vice* and *poison* which destroy the effect of all
" these *promising appearances !* To confirm this
" there is a passage cited from Plutarch (*De*
" *Orac. defectus*), which, being somewhat singu-
" lar, we shall here examine it."

" The author, endeavouring to account for the
" silence of many of the oracles, says that it may
" be ascribed to the *present desolation of the*
" *world*, proceeding from former wars and fac-
" tions ; which common calamity, he adds, has
" fallen heavier upon Greece than on any other
" country ; insomuch that the whole could
" scarcely at present furnish three thousand war-
" riors ; a number which, in the time of the

" Median war, was supplied by the single city of
" Megara. The gods, therefore, who affect works
" of dignity and importance, have suppressed
" many of their oracles, and deign not to use so
" many interpreters of their will to so diminutive
" a people."

" I must confess that this passage contains so
" many difficulties that I know not what to
" make of it! You may observe that Plutarch
" assigns for a cause of the decay of mankind,
" not the *extensive dominion* of the Romans, but
" the *former* wars and factions of the several
" States, *all of which were quieted by the Roman
" arms*. *Plutarch's* reasoning is, therefore, di-
" rectly contrary to the inference which is drawn
" (by Montesquieu) from the fact he advances."

Mr. Hume " does not know what to make of
this passage," and it must doubtless have appeared sufficiently perplexing and contradictory.
To the author, it seems to be (upon his own
principles) susceptible of a full and complete
explanation. Montesquieu, it appears, had arrived to full and sufficient knowledge of the FACT
that extensive and settled governments, and especially monarchies, which tend to encourage
luxury, and did not, in ancient times, *fiscally*
oppress the mass of the people, so as to drive

them to a poor and famishing manner of subsistence, are *not* favourable to population. This
fact the author of " The Spirit of Laws" had
satisfied himself was true; and therefore he
quotes Plutarch *for the fact*, that the population
of Greece had diminished from the period of its
conquest by the Romans down to his own time,
notwithstanding Plutarch himself attributes the
diminution to an opposite reason. That Plutarch
should reason differently is not surprising, though
his reason is a very unreasonable one, even upon
his own notions. It is difficult to bring men
in general to be convinced that a nation cannot
be permanently lessened by devastations through
war, so rapidly are the gaps in the population
filled up under such circumstances.

In more modern times we have seen the
history of the attempts to extirpate the Irish,
and have it recorded how rapidly their numbers
were recruited after a few years of respite and
repose. Plutarch, however, was not aware that
a people cannot be extinguished, unless by being,
as the Carthaginians were, brought into utter
slavery, and lost amid their conquerors; and
having also no conception of the truth which
President Montesquieu so confidently and properly enunciates, he had nothing for it but to

attribute the diminution of the Greeks to their *former wars;* which were constant enough, and cruel enough, and devastating enough; slipping over the difficulty that, during the long period which elapsed between the Roman Conquest and his own time, that is to say, between the taking of Corinth by the Consul Mummius, and Plutarch's time, a period of two hundred and fifty-six years, during which there were no devastations, a *cure,* upon *his own theory,* must have been surely wrought. This appears to the author to be a natural solution of the feelings and views under which both Montesquieu and Plutarch wrote. That the fact was as Montesquieu states, the author does not doubt. Though the Greeks, after the Roman Conquest, lost their independence, they were not oppressed. The ingenuity and industry of the people were allowed, in peace, to reap their own reward—comfort and affluence, and occasional luxury. Taxation was moderate, and being nearly altogether direct, trenched little upon the comforts of the mass of the inhabitants, and from the poverty and devastations caused by their own unruly passions, they were thenceforward exempt. Montesquieu is right, therefore, in attributing the thinner population to the Roman dominion ; and of the fact itself we cannot doubt, since Plutarch, who was himself a Greek, expressly states it, though he gives · the wrong reason for it. Their former numbers may have been exaggerated ; but of the general fact of the decay in their numbers, there seems to be no room for doubt.

Such were the opinions of the ancients as to the numbers of mankind at different periods. They certainly seem by no means to lean towards the recognition of any overwhelming tendency to constant growth ; but expressly recognise periods for decay and diminution, as well as periods for enlargement and increase. Nor are their statements to be set aside on account of occasional exaggeration, to which all computations as to numbers of people are peculiarly liable. If we come nearer modern times, we shall find the same opinions prevailing to more or less extent, as to certain periods, both of this country and others ; and probably not without foundation in truth.

Of all European countries, this opinion has been most prevalent with regard to Spain. If we are to believe the Roman writers, this fine and romantic country, when at last subdued by the wonderful military genius of Rome and her sons, was highly populous. Of what race the people were, is not at all clear. They are called by the Latin writers sometimes " Iberi," and sometimes " Hispani;" but the general opinion is, they were principally of the tribe called " Celts," who, leaving Asia at some remote period, as the spreading south-eastern population of that quarter of the globe began gradually to drive the more scattered, less dense, and more Nomadic tribes to the westward, spread themselves over Spain, then inhabited by the Iberi, Gaul, part of Germany, Belgium, and thence over to Great Britain and Ireland. From this singular race are supposed to be derived the Druidical monuments which exist in these islands; but the striking part of their character seems to have been their restless, untameable nature. Wherever they settled they seem to have been subdivided into small nations or clans, amongst which continued feuds and wars seem to have raged. This character seems to have attached to the Spanish part of them, who are always characterized by the Roman writers as a wrathful, quarrelsome, and ferocious race. " Impacatos Iberos" is Virgil's epithet for them, and the historians fully corroborate the Poet, painting them, one and all, as a bellicose race of savages, split into tribes, and making perpetual inroads upon each other's territory, much after the manner of the Highlanders of Scotland and the kings of Ireland, a very few centuries ago. Hume in his essay, as usual, takes this state to be one unfavourable to population ; but we have the direct testimony of history (Cicero de Haruspice, cap. ix.), that at this time the Iberian population was great. The Carthaginian inroads had not tended to alter the habits of the people ; and it was not until after they were completely subdued by the Romans, that their numbers began to decline. Nor is this wonderful, if we admit the truth of the theory here adduced. If, in modern times, we see a year of moderate dearness or scarcity, produce an immediate start in population (as has been shown in a preceding section), what must be the case when frequent devastations were producing artificial famines, and inducing perpetually recurring hardships amongst all classes of these people ? When Hispania, however, became a Roman province, it gradually became a rich country. That it was much cherished by the Romans, is a matter of history. Spain, until the discovery of Mexico and Peru, and the establishment of an intercourse with India, was almost the sole source whence the precious metals were obtained. Hence wealth flowed in, both upon the Roman conquerors and the inhabitants. Quiet and civilization went hand in hand with wealth; and after the spread of Christianity, Spain, owing to the romantic beauty of the country, became a favourite retreat for Christians who wished to escape in solitude from the sneers of the world, or perhaps its persecution. It was here that Ausonius addressed his deprecatory epistles to St. Paulinus, *(Ausonius, Epistolæ,* xxiv. xxv.) who had retired to this now quiet, civilized, moderately peopled, but still romantic country; and the sites of other hermitages are still pointed out in various parts of Spain and Portugal. About the year A. D. 409, in the general disruption of the Western Empire, this fine province was overrun by the Alanci, and other gothic hordes, who, following the early movement of the Celts, at last overwhelmed and trod to pieces the Roman Empire. To this succeeded the invasion and conquest of the Moors, until they again were finally driven out of Spain about A. D. 1312.

What might have been the population of Spain at the era of the expulsion of the Moors it is impossible to say, but it seems tolerably certain that the Spanish people have been since

that time declining in numbers rather than otherwise. From that time down to the present,
this singular and fine people have retained not
only their national habits, but their national
privileges.   Though united nominally in one
monarchy, the Basque provinces have retained
their language, their rights, and real independence.   They have never paid taxes beyond the
established fueros. Even Charles the Fifth, in
the plenitude of his power was compelled to
respect them, and their example has so far
operated, that it has preserved the rest of Spain
at all times from great Fiscal oppression, which
operates beyond all other causes put together to
alter the condition of a country long subjected
to it.   Hence wealth has been upon the whole
equably diffused through Spain, especially in the
Basque provinces, where nobility has no privileges.   Thus we see in Spain, as described by
Laborde and others, a fine and mountainous
country inhabited by a people for the most part
leading the pastoral life, and grazing herds of
cattle, sheep, goats, and swine, rather than employed in tillage, but caring little for commerce or
its products, save at the sea-ports and a few large
towns.   In such a country, divided for the most
part amongst small proprietors, who hand down

their little estates from generation to generation, the mode of living, though rough and simple, is plentiful and full. The vine sheds its blessings in the shape of the most nutritious wines over the whole region. The sugar of the raisin aids the fatness of the olive in producing a generous aliment for the cultivators of the soil and shepherds of the flocks and herds, which depasture in rich and endless droves in the rich valleys of this favoured land. Poultry is in abundance, and eggs, cheese, and butter add their nutriment to that derived from the flesh of cattle, sheep, and goats, with which the kingdom everywhere abounds. Travellers who talk of the poverty of Spain mistake roughness for want ; and wonder at finding bad inns amongst a pastoral people who care nothing for travellers. This equably diffused plenty the Spanish Monarchs have never been enabled materially to lessen by exactions ; and the political power of Spain, whilst she had political power, may be ascribed to the vast wealth which for a series of years the government derived from Mexico and Peru. That the influx of this wealth helped to check population still further, is evident in the fact, that Spain is now the least populous conntry in Europe ; and since the loss of the Indies, the most politically feeble, for with

that loss the revenue of the Monarch perished ,
and Spain, strong in herself, is powerless abroad.
Whilst Spain retains the olive and the vine, her
rich pastures and endless sheep-walks, her mag-
nificent woods, and arable plains, she can never
be populous, whilst peaceful and untaxed ; nor to
reverse such a state of things will a mere ordinary
warfare be sufficient, unless the devastations of
the Celts, and the perpetual strategy of the Iberi,
arise again to astonish modern times.

If we turn our attention to our own country,
we shall find the same notions of its former
populousness existing, and similar reasons for
believing them to be not unfounded in fact.
It has been supposed by many that, at the period
of the Norman Conquest, and during the times
anterior to that event, England had more inhabitants than she possessed some centuries afterwards ; nor are reasons wanting to prove the
probability of this opinion. If we look into the
details of the great battles fought, or armies
raised, from the period of the Conquest to the
time of Henry the Seventh, so far from finding
any superiority in the numbers of the more
modern armies, we discover the contrary, though
the kingdom was, during the latter period,
unquestionably richer, and the means for paying

and maintaining armies easier to be had. I
for instance, we are to credit history as to events
so comparatively recent as the Norman Invasion,
it seems undeniable that the armies commanded
by King Harold the Second at the battle of
Hastings, and the battle near York, which
immediately preceded it, must have been more
numerous than any army raised in England
from that time down to the conflict at Bosworth
Field, which gave the crown to Henry the
Seventh. In the battle at Stamford Bridge,
which immediately preceded that of Hastings,
Harold is said to have brought not less than
sixty thousand men to oppose Harfager, the
Norwegian Prince ; and Tosti, Earl of Northumberland, whose army, not much inferior to
Harold's, was partly composed of Englishmen.
In this bloody encounter, although victorious,
the English king's loss must have been severe ;
and yet eighteen days after this battle the fatal
conflict at Hastings is fought. In this great
conflict, it seems certain that the armies engaged
were superior in number to those who fought at
Stamford Bridge eighteen days before. William,
the Norman, had with him eight hundred and
ninety-six ships of all sorts ; which, at the rate
of eighty soldiers to each transport, gives an

armament of seventy thousand men. The English army, it is certain, though inferior in discipline, was superior in numbers, and if the impatient Harold would have waited for a few days, it would have been much more so. Though no quarter was given by the Normans, the number of English said to be slain is beyond all credibility, they being stated at sixty-seven thousand nine hundred and seventy-four men. It is quite certain, however, from the immediate submission that followed, that the slaughter must have been prodigious ; and it seems difficult to conceive that, on the English side, less than one hundred thousand men could have been engaged. If to these we add the numbers that must have been killed, wounded, and disabled, in many ways, at Stamford Bridge, eighteen days before, it makes the amount of Harold's disposable force very large ; and when in addition to this it is reflected that Tosti's troops were also Englishmen, we must conclude that not less than one hundred and fifty thousand Englishmen must have been engaged in these two encounters ; an enormous force, and not equalled in any action fought for many centuries afterwards in or by England.

If there be a period in which beyond all others

we should naturally look for a mighty prepara-
tion, that period is the date of Edward the
Third's French expedition. The nation was then
in a state of prosperity and wealth, which has
probably never really been exceeded at any future
time. As a proof of this, Rapin relates that a
private citiz n of London, a *wine-merchant*, at
the close of the war, entertained Edward, the
King of Cyprus, and the two kings of France
and Scotland, with all their attendants and the
whole court, in a most sumptuous manner. To
form an idea of what such of royal entertainment must necessarily have been we must turn
to Hollinshed, who, in his Chronicle, states
that, about this period, fifty-six different kinds
of foreign wine were drunk in England ! The
pay of Edward's army seems to have been upon a
scale according with this state of things : he had
introduced artillery, and the pay of some of his
gunners is put down at the enormous sum of a
shilling per day of the valuable money of that
time. The entire number of the army that
sailed with Edward was, however, only thirty-
one thousand six hundred and ninety-four men,
exclusive of the nobility, splendidly equipped,
no doubt ; but yet a small armament when com-

pared with those who fought at Hastings and
Stamford Bridge.

Later than this was the equally celebrated expedition of Henry the Fifth. As to the numbers
who attended him there seems to be less certainty. Rapin says fifty thousand men, but this
seems to include the sailors of the fleet, for
Monstrelet makes the fighting men amount to
only twenty-six thousand men. It seems clear,
however, that the number was not great, if we
are to believe the accounts as to the mere
handful that fought soon after at Agincourt.
The greatest battle after Hastings is however,
probably, Towton, in the next reign. In this
desperate conflict both sides were Englishmen;
the fate of the kingdom depended upon its issue;
the passions of both parties were roused to the
highest pitch; and it is probable that, as there
was ample time, every nerve was strained to
bring the greatest possible number into the field.
Yet giving all latitude to the accounts, it does
not seem that more than one hundred and eight
thousand men of all sorts met at Towton, when
both the North and South of England were
drained of all their men-at-arms for this grand
conflict. Here there is no symptom of increased

population, but the contrary. All the other Yorkist and Lancastrian battles were fought with very inferior numbers, and the slaughter seems to have fallen most upon the nobility and gentry, who were probably much more hearty in the cause than were the commonalty, who would understand little, and care less, about the dispute. It is to be remembered too, that these wars were spread over a period of from twelve to fifteen years.

Though the battle fought at Towton, in Yorkshire, was, in point of number, the greatest that was fought by the partizans of the Roses; yet both this battle, and that near Hexham, as well as at Hedgeley Moor, between Queen Margaret's forces and those of the Yorkists under Neville, Lord Montacute, and some others, of which part of the forces were derived from the North, show that, though there is no reason for supposing the population to be more than equal, or indeed quite equal to what it was at the period of the Norman Conquest, still that it had not declined in the marked and visible way in which it diminished after the reign of Edward the Fourth, which ended in 1483. We see here considerable forces raised in this part of the country, as far down as 1470. That the population had rapidly decreased after that time, is proved, not only by the Statute Book, but by such enumerations as took place after that period, within one hundred and fifty years. In 1615, it appears in Surtees' History of Durham" (vol. i., Appendix I., page cxxxvii.) that a muster of all males in the county of Durham, between the ages of sixteen and sixty, capable of bearing arms, was made on St. Giles-gate Moor, near the City of Durham, by command of the King, James I. The return is imperfect, the numbers for each parish being given for two of the four Wards only ; that is to say, for those of Easington and Chester. The totals, however, are given for the Wards of Darlington and Stockton ; so that we have the entire amount ; and the whole bears sufficient evidence upon it, that the muster and enumeration were made with an approximation to accuracy. This return would, of course, exclude the Clergy ; but it does not appear that there were any other persons exempt. The document is as follows :—

APPENDIX XXXIV.—(*Randall's MSS.*)

THE NUMBER OF MEN BETWEEN THE AGES OF SIXTEEN AND SIXTY, THAT APPEARED AT THE GENERAL MUSTER, ON ST. GILESGATE MOOR, A.D. 1615.

EASINGTON WARD.

St. Gyles' Parish	84
St. Nicholas	216
Hesleden	66
Easington	140
Trimdon and Kelloe	147
Aulton	51
Pittington	83
Houghton	289
Bishops-Weremouth	196
Lumley (part of Chester in Easington Ward)	80
Castle Eden	13
Seham	36
N. Bailey	54
S. Bailey	10
	1465

CHESTER WARD.

East Bolden	36
Monk-Weremouth	87
Whitburne	63
Washington	40
Jarrow	294
Gateshead	365
Lamesley	184
Ebchester	15
Carried forward	1084

Brought forward	.	.	.	.				1084
Ryton	.	.	.	.	.	.	.	277
Medomsley	.	.	.	.	.	.	.	53
Whickham	.	.	.	.	.	.	.	360
Lanchester	.	.	.	.	.	.	.	138
Eshe	.	.	.	.	.	.	.	20
St. Margaret's	.	.	.	.	.	.	.	187
St. Oswald's	.	.	.	.	.	.	.	119
Chester and Tanfield	.	.	.	.	.	.	.	239
Chapelry (qu. Satley)		.	.	.	.	.	.	72
Hunstonworth	.	.	.	.	.	.	.	14
Muggleswick	.	.	.	.	.	.	.	42
Witton Gilbert	.	.	.	.	.	,	.	44
Kibblesworth	.	.	.	.	.	.	.	8

2657

(TOTAL.)

Darlington Ward	.	.	.	2946
Stockton Ward	.	.	.	1223
*Easington Ward	.	.	.	1494
Chester Ward	.	.	°	2657

8220 persons.

Without supposing this document to be accurate, for of course there must have been numerous absentees, for various obvious reasons, it cannot still be doubted that it is an approximation to the truth, a second muster, two years after, being nearly the same.　Thus then we see, that in the space of about a century and a half, the

---

* This disagrees with the particular return.

whole of the men capable of bearing arms which the county of Durham could furnish, would hardly make a fifth part of those who perished on the side of the Lancastrians at the grand conflict of Towton, where the forces of Lancaster were drawn from the North. The slaughter of King Henry the Sixth's army at Towton, Dr. Lingard, a historian who is not disposed to exaggerate in these points, admits could not be much below thirty-eight thousand men, or nearly five times the Durham muster of 1615.

A more decisive testimony of the diminution of the population through the period that intervenes between the Norman Conquest and the reign of Elizabeth is, perhaps, the comparison of the ecclesiastical distribution of the country, which has existed since the Reformation, with that which had been made and existed for many centuries before that event. It is well known, that, let the distribution be made when it might, the parishes of England, up to the time of the Reformation, were much above thirteen thousand in number. In round numbers they may be stated at fourteen thousand. In each of these was resident a Rector or Vicar, who was not only maintained from the tithes, but was expected to show hospitality, and also to take care that the poor of his parish, if any, were relieved out of the tithes, of which they were held to be entitled to a share. After paying the poor and the Priest, the remainder went to build or repair the Church, and in part to the Bishop. That the tithes of all parishes were held to be amply sufficient for these purposes, is evident in the Act passed in the fifteenth year of Richard the Second, to compel the Monasteries who held livings to provide better for their Vicars (for thus came Vicars into the Church), and also to provide for the poor. The Statute enacts that " a convenient sum of money be paid and distributed yearly of the fruits and profits of the same Churches, by those that shall have the said Churches in proper use, and by their successors, to the *poor parishioners* of the said Churches, in aid of their living and sustenance for ever; and also that the Vicar *be well and sufficiently endowed.*" This Act, which is still law as far as vicarial tithes are concerned, was, as to the poor, of universal application to all parishes, and proves, as much as document can, that the thirteen thousand and odd parishes existing up to the time of Henry the Eighth, were cultivated, inhabited parishes; maintaining a Church, however small; and a priest, however poor; with some residue for destitute persons.

When, after the Reformation, the Church was remodelled, was it found necessary, in consequence of an exuberance of people, to divide populous parishes into two benefices, as might naturally be expected, if the people had exhibited any increase? Quite the contrary! After the Reformation, the number of benefices of all sorts, by moulding two livings into one in many cases, were reduced below the number of eleven thousand, and are at this moment only *ten thousand seven hundred and forty-two*, according to the return of the Government Commissioners, published "by command of his Majesty," in 1835. It is impossible to reconcile the new ecclesiastical distribution or division at the Reformation to common sense, unless upon the supposition that the hypothesis or supposition that the population had visibly decreased since the old division had obtained full credence. Had the extensive parishes become more populous, the course indicated was to divide further, and split the inconveniently populous into two. But the contrary course was taken. The conclusion therefore is, that a decreased population was apparent; for this

naturally leads to, and excuses a union of
parishes.

Upon a review of all these circumstances, it is
not easy to escape the conviction, that, from the
time of the Conquest up to Elizabeth's reign
inclusive, the population had not only been
stationary, but had at last declined visibly.
From the time of the Act of Parliament quoted
by Sir Frederick Morton Eden, up to the accession of James the First, in 1603, it seems
evident that the decay had been so visible as
to cause great alarm, though it had been less
palpable before that time. And, under the
theory here argued for, this was the natural
course of events. The country soon recovered
the effects of the Conquest ; the feudal institutions soon fell into desuetude ; and after the
extinction of the immediate Norman line, there
can be no doubt of the rapid progress of the
nation in wealth, power, and freedom. The
walled towns and sea-ports, one after another,
obtained charters ; Ireland was added to the
British dominions ; Wales was subdued ; France
was all but added to the Crown of England ;
Parliaments were free ; the old and mild common law of England was in full force ; trade
grew apace, and the nation, being free from a

foreign invader, and almost from a civil broil up to the reign of the Sixth Henry, had, beyond doubt, arrived at a pitch of generally diffused wealth, and even luxury, such as the world had not till then seen, nor perhaps dreamed of. Nor is it probable, on consideration calmly of the matter, that the general prosperity of the people suffered materially by the wars of the Roses. The parties unquestionably fought with great fury, and much blood was shed ; but the country was not devastated, as by a foreign invader. Neither party wished to injure nor exasperate the people, though they wished to put down each other ; hence, until the armies actually met, there was no hostility going on. They did not burn towns, nor lay waste the country, they only fought pitched battles in convenient positions. It is only by depressing for a length of time the social condition of large masses of people, that population is to be, or can be stimulated ; but this can only be done by a long series of hostile devastations, or by a continuous and grinding fiscal tyranny, reducing the mass of a people to live upon the lowest amount of sustenance upon which human life can be sustained. Hence, up to the period when the Reformation deprived the few poor in England of their share of the Church lands and tithes, want was unheard of, and the name of pauper unknown. That this happy state of society was not attended with an increasing population, but the contrary, the author trusts he has now adduced abundant evidence to prove.

That one of the causes of this happy and prosperous state, resided in the position of the Church at this period is, however, a truth that ought neither to be overlooked nor concealed. The Church was an easy landlord. It was her interest to attach the population to her; and hence her lands were always let upon long leases of lives, and at rates most moderate. That this acted generally upon the rates of rent cannot be doubted, although the immense rates of profit which all trades then enjoyed also had their share in keeping down the rentals of landed estates within very moderate bounds, compared with those of modern times. Thus the rental of land being moderate, and the population being moderate, and taxes and rates being almost unknown, the pay of the labourer was ample at the same time that the profits of traders were extraordinary. This is evident in the fact that agricultural labourers, whose statute wages were from *ninety to upwards of one hundred pounds a year*, in the money of this day, made to the sea-ports and walled towns, where higher rates were given! We can only judge of the profits of trade in these times by getting some idea of the *numbers* that were of one trade, and obtained a livelihood from it. To do this, there are no *data* remaining of the age of Elizabeth, as far as the author knows; but, going back even a century, the results are strikingly indicative. By the returns of licenses, it appears that in 1736, there were in London, of licensed houses for the sale of liquors, fifteen thousand eight hundred and thirty-nine. In 1835, only five thousand, with nearly three times the population. In 1785, the licensed soap-makers were nine hundred and seventy-one; in 1834 only three hundred and two. The soap made in 1785 was only *thirty-nine millions of pounds weight avoirdupois;* in the year 1835 *one hundred and fifty-four millions of pounds weight* were charged with, and the duty paid upon them. From this some judgment may be formed what the profits of trade must have been in the fourteenth and fifteenth centuries. The better, however, to assist this judgment, the author appends the following statement of the increase of the quantity, followed by a constant decrease in the numbers of manufacturers, which shews the rate at which profits have lowered and narrowed ever since 1785 ; and the reader may rest assured that the ratio *upwards*, is only the *inverse* of the ratio *downwards*.

STATEMENT.

(FROM PAGE 10 OF REPORT XVII. OF EXCISE COMMISSIONERS.)

Date	Hard Soap made.	Soft Soap made.	Number of Manufacturers.
1785	35,012,412lbs.	3,358,228	971
1790	42,074,309	3,671,425	772
1795	48,262,786	3,495,559	677
1800	54,233,311	3,528,432	652
1805	65,723,869	4,575,130	553
1810	72,636,296	6,146,529	510
1815	77,678,063	6,224,002	447
1820	82,379,891	7,099,297	398
1825	102,623,165	8,910,504	3 5
1830	117,324,321	10,209,519	309
1834	144,344,043	10,401,281	302

(The above was compiled from yearly returns.)

Another source of the ease and comfort of the people must not be passed over unnoticed ; and this source was comprised in the common lands. Up to the period of the Revolution of 1688, every township had its common, and every great town or borough its common, proportioned to the size and importance of the place. The use of these lands, it is clear, would fall mainly to

the share of the poorer inhabitants of the townships and of the borough towns; so that here
was another safeguard against destitution, of immense importance, if contemplated in its magni-
tude as a whole. It is impossible now to come
at any correct account of the extent of the common lands as they existed two centuries ago;
but some writers have not hesitated to estimate
them as high in amount as six millions of acres.
This may be, and probably is an over-estimate,
but that it is greatly over, the author does not
believe. If we take the parishes as they were
anterior to the Reformation, and allow three
townships to each country parish, this will give
a probable result of forty thousand townships,
after throwing off two thousand for the town
parishes. If each township had eighty acres of
common on the average, this would be three
millions and two hundred thousand acres, exclusive of the lands attached in the shape of common and moor to the great towns, the extents
of which were unquestionably very great. The
work of inclosing these commons under Acts of
Parliament, called Inclosure Bills, began in the
reign of Queen Anne, when three were passed.
The numbers increased slowly at first. George
the First assented to sixteen; and George the

Second to two hundred and twenty-three. After
the accession of George the Third, however,
inclosure of commons went on apace ; and in
his reign alone, three thousand eight hundred
and ninety-seven Inclosure Bills (or thereabouts)
were passed—(See Lords' Report, 1814, and
other documents)—so that the accounts up
to the accession of George the Fourth, stand
thus :—

		Bills for Inclosure.
Queen Anne	. . . .	3
George I.	. . . .	16
George II.	. . . .	223
George III.	. . . .	3,897
		4,139

Considering the numbers that must have
passed since, and considering the expenses of
local Acts, it seems probable that on the average
these bills must have alienated some hundreds
of acres for each bill. The former great extent of
the common lands, and the aid that the poorer
classes must have derived from them, become then
very apparent, and go to prove how impossible it
was, under all these concurrent circumstances,
that there should be anything like pauperism at
that time in England ; yet it is only since these

circumstances have been altered that fears of over-population have succeeded to the terrors of a decay of that, the rapid increase of which is now so greatly dreaded.

One more proof of the wealth of the times referred to, the author may adduce. This was the annual fairs, and the great importance attached to them. Every borough had by its charter one or two annual fairs, generally two ; one for cattle—one for merchandise. At these fairs it is known that the people universally not only bought their *annual stock* of many articles for ready money, but also cattle and swine to kill and salt for winter provision ; a fact which alone shows the ease in which they lived. These fairs exist in part now ; but the persons frequenting them are not the same, nor is the amount of lucrative traffic probably to be compared to that of former times, when all ranks bought and bought largely. Of such importance used these fairs to be, that when the City of Bath had Birton fair granted, the Burgesses of Bristol, out of jealousy, established a fair on the same day, and prohibited Bristol wares from going to Birton fair by a bye-law. On the Bathonians, however, petitioning the king (Edward III.), the evil was redressed by the king and Council. (Warner's History of Bath, p. 174.) Thus everything seems to concur to prove, at the period referred to, luxury and over-plenty wrought decay in numbers, and that it became at once necessary to pass statutes against luxury, and statutes to repair houses that were falling down for want of inhabitants.

CHAPTER XI.

CONSIDERATIONS OF THE INTERNAL EVIDENCE FOR THIS THEORY.

THE author of these sheets presumes that he may venture to lay down the following rule; that is to say, that whenever any theory or hypothesis as to natural dispensation or arrangement is, or can be shown to be, at apparent variance with the benevolence of the Deity, that variance is strong internal evidence against its truth, upon whatever grounds of proof of other descriptions such hypothesis may rest; whilst, on the other hand, it may be with equal fairness assumed, that when any hypothesis or scheme of natural arrangement or dispensation is in accordance with, and illustrative of, that benevolence which we attribute to the Deity as his personal attribute, then such accordance is,

quantum valeat, internal evidence of its truth—
that is to say, evidence as far as it goes—though
requiring the corroboration of other and more
direct evidence to amount to proof.   Thus, for
instance, when the existence of evil is supposed
as part of a hypothesis, without sufficient cause
in the shape of an ultimate beneficial result, or
without an evident necessity to preserve other
beneficial results already shown to be existing,
then this is indirectly to attribute the gratuitous
causation of evil to the Divine Being ; a position
at variance with the benevolence at first predi-
cated, which admits of the existence of evil only
because an imperfect state of being cannot admit
of a perfect state of happiness, but not of evil,
gratuitous, and arising neither from a necessity in
nature, nor as a means to a compensating beneficial end.

Having ventured these brief observations, the
author will now proceed to show that the hypothesis here advocated, is not liable to the objection
above stated, but is, on the contrary, entitled
to the benefit of such presumption in its favour,
as an accordance with the benevolence and
wisdom of the Divine Author of the Universe
is calculated to afford it, the natural arrangement it lays down being, if true and existing in

fact, apparently and plainly tending and intended to promote the happiness of mankind, with the causation of as little of accompanying evil as can well be conceived. In order to do this clearly and effectually, it is only necessary, first, to recapitulate the leading points or positions of the theory now attempted to be established; and then, having done this, to show the results, moral and physical, which flow from the admission of its truth. In the *first place* then, if this theory of increase and decrease be true, it is true that when any species, whether of the vegetable or animal kingdom, is endangered, by a failure or diminution of its natural sustenance, and reduced to the deplethoric state, then, in such case, is an immediate stimulus given to increase, which continues as long as the state continues. *Secondly*, it is also true, that if on the contrary, such species shall receive immoderate natural aliment, and be brought into the extreme plethoric state, then, in that case, increase is immediately checked, and decrease takes place, which continues as long as the state is continued. *Thirdly*, it is also true, that if moderate sufficient aliment, or a moderated plethoric state, is allotted to, and brought upon any species, then mere reproduction will be the result, without increase or decrease of existing numbers. *Fourthly*, that if equal portions of the same species be put into these different states, in equal degrees, it follows, as a true conclusion, that the decrease of one portion will be compensated by the increase of the other, and numbers remain as they were. These four propositions, the author trusts he has in the foregoing sections of this work given evidence to establish ; and supposing the theory which they embody to be true, let us now inquire into the different results, natural and moral, which flow from them.

The first consideration likely to attract the attention of the reader is, as it seems to the writer, that under this law of increase and decrease, a provision is made for the protection of any species that is endangered, which is efficient only *when* it is wanted, and in the precise *ratio* in which it is wanted. This, upon the face of it, seems surely to be a more wise and providential arrangement, than would be a law under which the tendency to increase is supposed to be always equal. It is so, because such a law as that presupposes an equal protection equally requisite at all times, which is absurd. If we take the evidence of facts, and look round us, we shall find that such is not the case. The course of nature is one of constant change and vicissitude; and this being so, it follows that whether we look at the vegetable or animal kingdom, there must be times when existing species are more endangered than they are at other times. In times of dearth, flood, and pestilence, species must be more endangered than during genial and healthy periods. This seems undeniable; and being so, it follows that any unvarying law of increase would be inapplicable ane absurd; because it might be barely sufficient for the exigence at one time, and ridiculously superfluous at another. It is not easy to conceive, that the Creator should so order as to let a species be destroyed for want of a sufficient protective law at one season or time, and at another force on a superfluity of existence, to be destroyed again from want of sustenance, without the slightest conceivable reason for so doing. In short, the supposition of such a law is to suppose the application of an invariable rule to ever-varying circumstances, which is an absurd supposition, and not in accordance either with the wisdom or benevolence of the Deity; whilst a law that is efficient when wanted, and which is relaxed when not wanted, seems to be in strict accordance with a providential wisdom and benevolence, and equally well calculated for the protection and benefit of created beings, of whatsoever description they may be. In short, as it seems to the author, a law such as he has described seems to unite the two desirable attributes of being, not only beautiful as an arrangement, but benignant as an instrument.

If, looking at the opposite effect of the law of increase and decrease now enforced, we consider the consequences of an arrangement for diminution and check at certain times, as well as for increase at others, we shall find them also to be plainly beneficial, and calculated to attain a desirable end. The author must admit, and he readily does so, that he is not prepared to state, with regard to the vegetable creation, what the effect of the highly plethoric state is upon the health of a plant. By analogy, however, it may be presumed to be probably injurious ; because if we look at the animal kingdom, as far as we have tolerably precise and minute knowledge, we find the highly plethoric state always injurious to the health of the animal. In the human animal, luxuriousness and over-feeding is generally admitted by physiologists and physicians to be the root of most organic diseases. With regard to domestic animals the same truth is undeniable and easily perceptible ; and if we seldom witness it in animals not domestic, it is because their food is in general probably only apportioned to the labour they must undergo to procure it, and because our opportunities for observation are also few. Reasoning, however, upon what we do know, it is not difficult to perceive the wisdom of a check to propagation under circumstances of extreme luxuriousness, because by this provision the transmission of organic disease is avoided. Thus, under this arrangement, let the danger come from which side it may, it is guarded against, and the species preserved from the risks of destitution or want of sustenance on one hand, and the perils of an unhealthy luxury on the other. Assuming this explanation of the providential benefit of the check here described to be the true explanation, it seems an inference highly probable, that to the vegetable tribes the high stimulus of over sustenance and the effects of repletion are as injurious as to the animal. This is probable as an inference, because in the vegetable kingdom the check to propagation is as invariably and more rapidly applied when a state of repletion is induced in the plant, than it is to the living animal. Flowers, shrubs, and trees, planted in soils much too rich for them, almost immediately suffer, and cease to bear. In the flowers the leaf becomes double, and the organs of reproduction are obliterated or injured. In trees the blossom is deficient and unfruitful. To suppose so marked an effect as this without a reason for it, is much the same as to suppose an effect without a cause, or that physical causes are not always accompanied by moral reasons— an idea faulty and untenable in itself, and repugnant to the infinite wisdom and prescience of the Creator.

Such are the beneficial consequences, as to the preservation of created beings of every species, of the arrangement here insisted upon ; but if the author were to stop here, he would, as it seems to him, leave untouched a most interesting and extensive branch of this part of his subject, and fall short of the moral purpose which ought to form at least one of the motives to all sorts of literary composition. We have ascertained thus far how beneficially, as to the physical welfare of created existences, this scheme seems to be calculated to work ; but on its tendencies and effects as to the well-being and government of nations, we have not touched. It comes next in order, to inquire, if this theory be true in fact, how and in what manner its natural consequences may be supposed to act upon the social condition of mankind, and upon the welfare of man as collected into communities of individuals, whose conduct separately, has a certain action upon the happiness of the whole. Let us make this inquiry.

If it be true, as the author is well convinced it is, that population is checked or increased according to varying or opposite circumstances, it follows as a plain consequence that a community may suffer in two different ways, or from two opposite mistakes, as to their social condition. If, for instance, a nation be so circumstanced that its population has a general command, not only over the necessaries, but also over the luxuries of life, it may still happen that, whether this command be the fruits of mild and good government, or of great industry, or of peculiar position, or a combination of all or some of these advantages, this apparently fortunate situation may in the end be unfortunate if these advantages be abused. Evil may here arise out of a very superfluity of good; for if the bulk of a people indulge in luxury to an excess, the consequence must be, not only an effeminacy of mind and morals, and a decay of the public virtues which are necessary to the existence of states, but, in addition to this, an actual physical decay and diminution of numerical strength, probably most rapid at the top of society, and extending downward as far as the luxury reaches in the ratio of its extent. Such States soon become the prey of other States, whose situation has not possessed the same tendencies towards national debility, or become the victims of some tyranny within themselves, which, in either case, works a sharp and bitter cure to an insidious disease. Such, beyond a doubt, is the true history of the fall of many States. It was probably the too great luxury which grew up in England under the Dynasty of the Plantagenets, which lulled the English people into their submission to the vices and tyrannies of the Tudors. Thus, if we knew the particulars, in all probability fell the Assyrian Empire; and by this process most certainly came the ruin of that of Rome. Let us glance rapidly over the circumstances, and we shall soon be convinced of this. During the earlier period of the Republic the same severe simplicity of life pervaded all ranks; and hence all ranks contributed their share to the strength and growth of the state. The consuls, generals, judges, and priesthood, were generally of the Patricians; the soldiers, the cultivators, and the skilled in the useful arts and handicrafts, were the free citizens of Rome and her Republic. The gradual inroads of a more luxurious state of society, however, gradually altered this state of affairs, until, even in the time of the Gracchi, the decay of free Roman citizens in the provinces, and the increase of the lower and slave population, induced the two brothers to struggle for a revival of the ancient Agrarian Laws, and a better allotment of the tributary lands and territories. The degenerate republic was at last subverted, but under the empire, luxury still grew ; and the end was, after many centuries, that the empire, both of the West and East, left to mercenaries for defence, crumbled under the blows of the Goths, Huns, and Ottomans, until there remained not even the shadow of a name. The fall of the luxurious Eastern Empire was characteristic. For years before the final doom, the entire population almost, of what was called the Eastern Empire, was gathered into a space consisting of the City of Constantinople, and a territory of about seven broad miles round the walls ! They had, when their mercenary soldiers failed them, bought truce after truce, of their Ottoman invaders, until they had nothing left but the city and its treasures, and themselves, to give. Mahomet the Second stormed the city, and one day (the 29th of May, 1453,) sufficed to tread out the last sparks of the Roman Empire and its once omnipotent people. In this, and in other catastrophes of a similar kind, we see the origin of the notion of Montesquieu, that absolute monarchies contained in themselves some hidden and mysterious principle of decay, which was sure in the end, to bring them to destruction. The assertion is correct, though he was ignorant of the steps of the process. He had failed to perceive the manner in which the exuberance of too great an abundance saps a population. It begins, like Tarquin in his garden, by thinning the tallest poppies, and so proceeds downwards through the whole diseased community. But the strength of monarchical and aristocratic governments lies in the upper and middle ranks. In these must reside the spirit of rule, which is to keep the empire together; and when these decay, the empire itself decays with them, for the military and domestic serfs are nearly, at last, all that is left; and deprived of their natural leaders they soon become inefficient or dangerous. So rapid was the decline in Rome, that though Julius Cæsar, to recruit the extinct nobility, ennobled a vast number of families, it

was found requisite to repeat the operation by
the Emperor Claudius ; and soon after that time,
we find Juvenal, in his Sixth Satire, hinting,
and more than hinting, that, were it not for
the amours of the Roman ladies with their slaves,
and the palming of supposititious children upon
their husbands, many of the noblest families
would be without an heir !

" Nobilis Euryalum Mirmillonem exprimat infans !"

is one of his lines. It requires two of English
to do it justice.

" How sweetly marked the noble infant shews,
Euryalus the Sworder's mouth and nose !"

Enough, however of this part of the subject.

If in those portions of this theory which
exhibit the effect of luxury carried to excess
amongst a people, may be discovered a political
lesson, by no means to be despised, we may
derive one fully as important from those other
portions of it, which go to explain the effects,
upon population of the opposite state of general
destitution.

From this operation of the Law of Population
may be deduced one grand and salutary axiom,

and that is, that a long-continued depression, down to destitution, of a whole people, will, in the long run, be revenged on itself and those who caused it, by the superfluous and unmanageable pauper population which it is sure to generate. From the same facts, also, we may draw another axiom, not less important; and this other axiom is, that no kind of misgovernment is so dangerous and fatal as a fiscal tyranny, whether such tyranny consists in the prostration of the poor cultivators before the rapacity of the owners of the soil, or before the united exactions of government and landlord. In either case the fruit is, at last, an overwhelming and starving population, for which society cannot find either room, food, or employment, and who are, therefore, perpetually urged, by necessity and the pangs of hunger and want, to overset the government which has been the means of creating and placing them in this dreadful situation. It is very clear that this description of oppression is infinitely more fatal and prolific of evil than were any of the ancient tyrannies, dreadful as some of them were. This is because their oppressions fell more upon individuals than upon classes. If a subject grew too rich, they robbed him; if if he resisted, they murdered him; and what

they coveted, they took. But elaborate misgovernment requires civilization as well as elaborate good government; and this point they never
reached. Their taxation was direct and simple,
not indirect and complex. Hence, however
heavy, it fell mostly upon the richer classes, and
no extensive masses of men were or could be
driven by it into destitution. To do this, the
multiform pressure of indirect taxation is necessary, which, by laying its imposts upon the
articles of daily consumption, causes a people to
pay imperceptibly some fiscal tribute upon every
morsel, drop, or rag, which they eat, drink, and
wear, as each article is consumed.

The system of serfdom and vassalage also, with
all its evils, interposed between the serf and the
vassal and his lord, by the very act of making
them an actual property; and the Persian satrap,
the Roman patrician, knight, or landowner, as does
the Russian nobleman, reckoned his serfs amongst
the number of his cattle, and took care of their
welfare upon the same principle that he took
care of his other live stock. Hence, slaves are
fully fed, whilst free labourers, as they are called,
are often starved; because the master has a
property in the first, which he has not in the
last. If a man kills his slave, he has another to

buy, as well as to find him victuals when he is
bought. When a free labourer pines and dies,
the master has only to offer the same wages, and
the place is filled up. Who would care to lose a
horse if another walked into the stable free of
cost, and was ready to serve for the same
pasturage (how poor soever) as the last had.
Thus, therefore, the very fact of being a distinct
property, ameliorated the condition of the serf,
and kept down their numbers ; and hence it is,
that hateful as feudal tyranny may be called,
fiscal tyranny is still worse ; both, ultimately, for
those who oppress and those who are oppressed ;
inasmuch as the few oppressing thousands must
be perpetually in risk from the starving and
increasing millions.

Having gone into the foregoing considerations,
as being the most obvious, first ; the author will
now turn to another view of some of the
conclusions deducible from this theory, which,
placing as it does, the moral government of God
in the world in a new and original light, may be
presumed neither to be uninteresting nor unim-
portant. If we examine the infinite varieties,
shades, and grades of the human character, we
can hardly avoid coming to this conclusion, that
there cannot (let theorists and visionaries dream

as they will) be possibly such a state as that of equality of *conditions* throughout a country, or throughout the world. As long as men are endued with various degrees of talent, courage, industry, perseverance, frugality, generosity, foresight, virtue, and prudence, so long, as it seems to the author, must their worldly conditions vary. The prudent man will save more than the dissolute; the adventurous man grasp more than the timid; the persevering man will succeed after the timid has failed; the virtuous man will retain what the vicious man will squander; the overreaching knave will rob the simply honest; the cunning gamester will outwit the wild spendthrift; the sagacious schemer will outstrip the simple plodder; and the innate miser will save what the generous and humane give away. Thus, then, inequality of physical condition seems a part, and no doubt a necessary part, of the scheme of Divine Providence; for it is impossible to separate inequality of mental gifts from inequality of physical results and consequent conditions. Nor is this distribution difficult to be accounted for under the benevolent scheme of a Divine Providence; when it is considered that the stimulus of bettering our condition may be one of the motives necessary to the

complete exertion of all our faculties, and be as
requisite to the action of society as is the spring
to the watch, or the oxygen of the blood to the
motion of the heart.   Still, after giving due
weight to all these considerations, it cannot be
denied, that, upon the ordinary view taken of
this arrangement, there yet remained a ground
for cavil and for repining.   Still it was asked,
why should so large a share of the goods of the
earth be given to one class, and denied to those
below them ?   It bore the appearance of an
unfair monopoly.   Here was a limited class of
mankind handing down, as was commonly supposed, immense possessions to their posterity,
unless some strange and equally to be deprecated
violence interfered to change the transit, and
despoil the heir of his wealth.   From this objection it is difficult to escape, if the ordinary
notion as to the progress of population be once
admitted.   Under the theory now brought forward, however, this objection vanishes, and the
most equable distribution possible, under a
system in which inequality at all is necessary,
is proved to prevail.   For if we look at society
and its progress, as here described, we find that
all increase is from beneath, and all decrease
from above.   The holders of wealth cannot

maintain a posterity long to which to transmit it.
Even " *old* families," as is beautifully said by Sir
Thomas Browne, " do not last *three oaks !*"
Hence the descendants of the poor, in an unbroken succession, are continually inheriting the
possessions of the rich; and instead of being
entailed upon a class, they in a perpetual routine
fall to the lot of those to whom a country owes
its increase of people—the poor, and the descendants of the poor. Thus, though there is
individual inequality, there is no other inequality.
The offspring of the poor inevitably, in process
of time, become possessed of the accumulations
of the rich ; and then, in their turn, yield them,
for want of heirs, to the children of those who
have not yet become rich ; a distribution so
beautifully equitable, in the midst of apparent
inequality, as to be calculated to excite the
deepest admiration of all reflective minds. Whether riches, as some suppose, give happiness,
or, as others suppose, the reverse, it is clear the
happiness or the misery is not the heirloom of
a single class, but falls, in turn, to the lot of
individuals of all classes ; an equal distribution,
and worthy of that Creator who, out of seeming
disorder, can produce order, and is always found
to do so, when man can scrutinise his ways.

As some further corroborative proof of the truth of this view of the matter, the author may observe, that the estates which have most constantly descended in a long, unbroken, and direct line, from father to son or daughter, are supposed to be those small freehold farms, the property of the class known in England as the " yeomen," a class of men just wealthy enough to be happy, but not to be luxurious nor idle. In Cumberland and Westmoreland they were once numerous ; and some exist still, which have been for centuries in the hands of one family. In Spain, especially in the Basque Provinces, they are numerous at this hour. Each possesses its substantial, but small, stone antique mansion ; and to see their fertile valleys, studded with these houses, in the midst of beautiful pastures, tilled lands, vineyards, orchards, and groves of olives, is a sight which, to the eye of reason, outvies all the splendour of this world, and realises, after the Fall, the nearest conception we can form of the Paradise before it.

The author now concludes. It has been his aim throughout the foregoing sheets, not only to demonstrate what is the nature of the laws which regulate the increase and decrease of population, but also to show that these laws are beautiful in their arrangement; that they are calculated to promote the happiness of mankind in their action; that any deviation from the course which they indicate to society as being proper to be pursued, is immediately or ultimately, but most assuredly, punished in its own after effects; and that the whole theory of population, as it exists in facts, is worthy of the benevolent wisdom of God, and in perfect accordance with His good providence as displayed in the other parts of our mundane economy. The accidental circumstances which led the writer of these sheets into the course of reasoning which he has attempted to follow out, he has detailed in a concluding chapter, deeming that method upon the whole, and for the reasons assigned, preferable to interweaving any account of them in the foregoing pages. His argument ends here; and he was unwilling to embarrass it with anything extraneous, or of a merely collateral and perhaps questionable character. Whether he has succeeded or failed in his present attempt his readers will judge. If he be considered to have failed in his undertaking, he hopes to that failure will not be added the accusation of anything of arrogant assumption in his manner of pursuing it. If, on the other hand, he may, happily, be judged to have succeeded, as he would fain flatter himself he has done, he humbly trusts he may be classed amongst those who are held to be not unworthy of the sympathy of their fellows, and may be esteemed to have passed through life not undeserving of the respect of mankind.

CHAPTER XII.

SOME ADDITIONAL COLLATERAL CONSIDERATIONS, AND ADDENDA.

IN writing this concluding chapter the author would, in the first place, wish it to be distinctly understood that these paragraphs form no part of his argument, nor are they intended to form any part of it. Many of the topics now touched upon are altogether extraneous : others have merely a collateral bearing upon the subject in question ; and many of them are in themselves, as the author is well aware, extremely doubtful and questionable. Notwithstanding this, it seemed to the writer of these pages, upon the whole, useful, and not improper to give some account of the accidental circumstances which directed his mind to that course of inquiry which it ultimately followed. These circumstances are in themselves not uninteresting, because they are somewhat singular; and though the considerations which arise out of some of them may not bear directly upon the question at issue, they yet bear upon it indirectly and collaterally, and, though in themselves doubtful, and only adduced as such in these pages, they are yet curious, and not unworthy, perhaps, of the attention of the physiologist or general inquirer into nature, of whatever name or description. It is proper to add, however, that in noting down, as he is now about to do, the peculiar circumstances which led him to the present inquiry, and the different views and conclusions, arrived at with more or less of doubt, which forced themselves upon his mind during its course, the author by no means wishes to assume to himself credit for any general knowledge of physiology or natural history. Quite the contrary. In truth, his knowledge of this class of subjects of human inquiry is extremely limited, and altogether imperfect; and he consequently deems no other of the ideas that have occurred to him as worthy of preservation, than as notions rather forcing themselves upon, than sought by a mind accidentally engaged in a course of inquiry foreign to its usual pursuits. The particular circumstances which led to the first

conception, and ultimate completion of the foregoing attempt, were as follows :—

Some years ago, the author of these sheets
being (as has been already intimated) attached in
some measure to gardening pursuits; being also
early compelled, by the nature of his trade, to
have some general knowledge of chemistry, and
its more ordinary results ; and having ample
opportunities to put his inclinations into practice, amused himself with a few experiments to
ascertain, if possible, the substance or substances
which constitute the basis or stimulating principle of manures. It always was, and is still his
opinion, that our knowledge of manures, and the
modes of their application in agriculture and
horticulture, is completely in its infancy. He
has long considered the knowledge of the moving
principle of cultivation ; that is to say, the
accurate knowledge of the precise substances in
which the vegetative stimulus actually resides,
to be itself an uncultivated field ; and, this being
the case, it was not extraordinary that he should
break ground in a quarter, where, as so little
had been done, so much might be expected.
From a promising soil, where the surface has
scarcely been broken, the cultivators, however
unskilful, naturally expect good returns ; and

such, probably, was the reasoning, and such were the motives that led to a series of experimentings, which, if they have produced little else, have, at all events, produced this book !

In pursuance of his course of experiments the author was, of course, led by the nature of his pursuit, to apply various substances which he either knew, or deemed likely, to contain in themselves, in combination, the active principle of manure, to various trees, plants, shrubs, and flowers, and to note the results. During this process, one result became, at last, strongly indicated to his mind; and this was, that, whatever might be the principle of manure, or the substance that contained it, an OVERDOSE of it invariably induced sterility in the plant, and, if the dose were increased, disease and death. When trees were overstimulated by manures they made a superfluity of wood, blossomed extremely scantily, and only towards the extremities of the branches, in situations farthest from the root; and finally, the blossoms rarely set, or produced ripe and perfect fruit. In cases of flowering shrubs, the same defect of flowers followed, and with annuals and other flowers, the flower frequently became what is called double, and ceased to seed. To recover trees treated in this way, it became necessary to put an end to the overstimulus caused by the extra dose of manure by a reversed process. The tree was to be debilitated to a certain extent, and ringing the bark, extreme lopping, and trenching the roots, were the expedients. With plants and flowers a similar process of check or depletion, either by lopping, or, if greenhouse plants, by exposure to cold, was successful. The checked and debilitated plant flowered plenteously after a state of depletion ; and the tree, after being lopped and ringed, began to bear. That the perfect indication of this law, in the increase or decrease of the vegetable creation, should lead the writer onward to an extended inquiry, was not only not unnatural, but almost inevitable. He was naturally induced to ask if the same regulation extended through animated nature, and pursuing the inquiry, he found that it did so ; that it pervaded the animal creation ; and finally, was applied by his Creator to man himself. Still, in the midst of all the various phenomena, either indicated by actual experiment, or narrated by the various writers on physiology or nosology, which the author was induced to read, he found little or nothing to indicate the *modus operandi*—that is to say, the manner or mode by which sterility in one case, or fecundity in the other, was brought about. That sterility in the human female was the frequent consequence of plethora, whether *positive* or *relative*—for so medical writers divide it—and that fecundity constantly followed the opposite state, he met with abundant evidence to show. To physicians and anatomists, however, the immediate and proximate causes of sterility, or its opposite, appear to be as great a mystery as they are to the writer of the foregoing chapters. Thus, the writer of the article " Impotence," in the " Cyclopædia of Medicine," says, "In the city (Dublin), where misery, poverty, and starvation exist, to a degree perhaps unparalleled on the face of the globe, *procreation proceeds with extraordinary rapidity;* and it has fallen to the writer's lot, through his connexion with the Coombe Lying-in Hospital, to witness the birth of numberless infants, whose unfortunate parents had *not for years partaken of a wholesome meal.*" Here we have evidence of the fact of starvation and fecundity going on hand in hand ; on this point the writer is decisive ; but of *the mode* by which Nature causes prolificness in the female to be a consequence of a constant state of depletion, he gives no hint. The same knowledge of the fact, joined with the same ignorance of the

mode, is evinced by those writers who adduce
barrenness as one consequence of a state of
plethoric in the human female. Thus Doctor
Combe, in his work " on Digestion and Dietetics,"
gives the following instructive statement :—" A
young woman of a healthy constitution, brought
up in all the simplicity of country habits, passed
at once, on her marriage, to a *less active mode of
life*, and to a *much more elegant table*. In a short
time she began to complain of irritability,
lassitude, various spasmodic sensations, and
habitual constipation. *Hypochondria* was soon
added to the other symptoms. *Her hope of be-
coming a mother being always deceived*, an *additional* glass of wine, bark, and other tonics
were ordered : the evil increased. The patient
became *melancholy*, and believed that she was
always swallowing pins. In the course of the
year she became so emaciated and yellow that
her mother, who had not seen her for eleven
months, could scarcely recognise her. After an
eighteen months' course of purgatives, and two
courses of Marienbad water, she *entirely recovered*." Here is evidence of the *fact*, and of
the strongest sort ; for the plethoric state here
induced was " relative," and not " positive."
The appearance of a healthy obesity, which is

" positive plethora," was not induced. The functions of life were, however, disordered to a great extent—disordered and clogged ; the biliary, digestive, and excretory vessels could not act; and, as it should seem, those more minute ducts, on the free action of which conception by the female seems to depend, were partakers of the general constitutional derangement, arising from this overloading of the system. And here the author would respectfully ask those qualified by education and knowledge to answer such a question, what is there extraordinary in this ? If a state of plethora can, as it is held it can, prevent the action of a gland or of a viscus, why should it not be a sufficient cause for the inaction of that finer and more minute apparatus upon the unimpeded state of which must, probably, depend the transit of the ovum from the ovarium to the uterus ; or what of improbability is there in the supposition, that, during a state of unnatural obesity and repletion, this must be the case, and *vice-versa ?* These are of course questions for the anatomist and physiologist alone ; and, in suggesting them, the author would only guard those who treat of this subject, from confounding with a state of true plethora, that apparent pinguetude, or bloatedness of fibre,

which is a frequent accompaniment of debility,
especially in the strumous constitution, which
most writers hold to originate in debility—the
consequence of deficient nourishment, and an
unnatural state of depletion.

So much for the possible proximate causes of
sterility in the female; but there is, perhaps,
another cause of want of offspring, which may
be referred to the male constitution as acted upon
by diet, and to which, if indeed it be a cause, the
author was led by some of the results of those
experiments to which he has already alluded.
After submitting growing vegetables to the action
of various substances, known, or supposed to be
" manures," he at last arrived at one general
conclusion ; and this was, that all substances that
contain portions, that is to say, sensible or considerable portions of any of the alkalies in combination with their other constituents, may be expected to act, and will, generally speaking, act as
manures.   It is not intended to be argued that
their effect as manures is in the exact *ratio* of
the alkali present.   The results are, and
evidently must be, modified in many ways.   One
compound may be more easily decomposed than
another when in contact with the roots of the
plant.   The components of the original soil may

accelerate or retard this decomposition, as their nature may happen to be. The presence of lime, chalk, gypsum, or of strata, containing marine shells, or other marine deposits, is almost certain to produce some effect upon chemical action. To produce a manure there must be present one or more of the alkalies, and hence all ordinary substances in which soda, potass, or ammonia, are known to be constituents, chemically act as manures. Thus the dung of all animals; the bodies of animals, wood ashes, the cinders and ashes of coal, bones, calcined sea-weed, the waste ashes of the soap-boiler, the suds of soap, common salt, saltpetre or nitrate of potass, nitrate of soda, the decomposed bodies of fish, and the horny parts of animals, as well as their skins, are all found to act as manures, with more or less of success according to the other accompanying circumstances. Thus far the experiments made by the author invariably led, when other circumstances occurred which took him one step further, that is to say, to the belief that the alkali when it acts as a stimulant is *caustic*, or in part so. To this conclusion he came from observing the following circumstances :—In order to ascertain, if possible, the true effects of soda as a manure, he applied to the roots of several bulbous plants, by dissolving in the water in which they grew, minute quantities of pure carbonate of soda. In the first set of experiments so tried, the effect upon the flower was extraordinary; it was not only doubled, but, to use a strong phrase, tripled and quadrupled, until in more than one instance the structure of the flower, to an ordinary observer, was totally altered. A second set of experiments tried at another place, however, produced no such results. The carbonate of soda, when in solution as before, hardly stimulated the plant, even when the quantity was increased, and it became evident that something remained to be accounted for. The author at last satisfied himself that the discrepancy arose from the circumstance of the water first employed holding *lime* in solution, whilst the water last employed was destitute of it, and in every way much purer and more free from extraneous substances. Hence the carbonate of soda, in the first experiment, gradually parted with its carbonic acid, and became caustic; whilst in the last, nothing being present which had a greater chemical affinity for carbonic acid, no causticity took place.

Thus, then, the conclusion was arrived at, that caustic and pure alkali is the basis, or rather

stimulative principle of *manure*. It is the principle which causes the seed to expand, the plant
to push, and the work of vegetable growth to
proceed. Whether the plant itself possesses the
property of slowly decomposing, and obtaining it
from the substances which hold it in combination,
is a question to be solved. One thing seems to
be certain, that where it is present in quantity,
if it be not in excess, vegetation is stimulated by
it. Pursuing the inquiry upwards, from the
vegetable to the animal kingdom, the next question is—may not that which stimulates the *seed*
into life, stimulate the *egg* into life ; and may not
one law, here, run throughout nature ? In
answer to this inquiry, there are certainly some
facts that speak strongly in the affirmative ; and
these are, that alkali, that is to say *soda*, is found
in the albumen of the eggs of birds, and also in
company with *ammonia* in the " liquor seminalis"
of animals, including man. Fourcroy, in his
analysis of the " liquor seminalis" of a healthy
man, detected both caustic soda, and ammonia
in quantity ; and since his time the presence of
active alkali in this secretion, has been placed
beyond all doubt or question. Thus, then, there
is ground for the supposition, at all events, that
the neutralization, or absence of alkali, in the

male animal constitution, would be a direct cause of sterility, and its decided presence, *e contrario,* a cause of fruitfulness ; supposing, in each case, the female to be prolific by constitution. Thus then, we come, as it were insensibly, to the consideration of the final step of this question, which is, whether the states which have been proved to be favourable or unfavourable to fecundity amongst mankind, are favourable or unfavourable to the development, in the constitution of the male, of those substances which are probably necessary to procreation ? What is the tendency of an animal, or plethoric diet, as to the constitution ? What is the tendency of a vegetable, or deplethoric diet, as to the constitution ? In the answers to these questions will reside the proof of the probability or improbability of the foregoing considerations.

Now, then, if we examine the writings of the principal medical and dietetic authors, such as Majendie and others, we shall find the prevalent opinion to be, that a plethoric diet, that is to say, a diet of animal food and wheaten bread, with wine and sugar in combination, liquid or solid, is accompanied by a development of *acid* in the frame ; whilst, on the contrary, a poor, unwholesome, deficient, or indeed mostly vegetable nutriment, tends rather to an *alkalescent* state of the body, from which acid is excluded. Of the true piethoric habit, the presence of severe and constantly recurring gout, is perhaps the most unerring symptom; and in this disease the development of acid is so striking, as not to be mistaken. The urine is overloaded with it, both previously to, and during the fit. It forms deposits of chalkstones upon the joints, in combination with lime, which it obtains from the blood, or from the bone itself; and so predominant is it, that in severe fits, the vegetable blues are turned red, when touched with the perspiration of the inflamed part. On the contrary, sea scurvy, the most dreadful disease caused by deficient and unwholesome nutriment, is known in its last stages, to produce a highly alkalescent state; so much so, that " the urine turns blue vegetable infusions to a green colour." It may be indeed objected, that fruits and vegetables help to cure this disease; but this is clearly from their containing more or less of acid, which at once neutralises the alkali. Thus *citric-acid pure*, if administered, produces immediate relief. The cure, however, is only to be performed by administering with acids, nutritious and quickly digestive articles of diet. Hence *sweet-wort* is sovereign in cases of scurvy, as are whey and other diluents containing sugar, which of all nutriment is most concentrated and easy of digestion. Fresh animal food also is proper, for it is only from the use of meat that has lost all its nutritious qualities that the disease is engendered, increased, probably, by the salt with which the meat is cured.

Thus, then, a state of plethora, whether it is considered as acting mechanically or chemically upon the human frame, is probably indicative of barrenness or paucity of offspring. The state of depletion and debility, on the other hand, appears both chemically and mechanically to be favourable in its effects, both upon the male and female organization, to fecundity, or excess of offspring. That the considerations upon which this conclusion is founded, are of a general and vague nature, the author readily admits. They do not however, seem to be contradictory to any received facts, either of anatomy or nosology, but are upon the whole borne out by the writings of those versed in both. The conclusions which the author has deduced from them are in themselves general, and he trusts he has not laid upon them more weight than the premises are calculated to carry; at all events, it is by no means his wish that his readers should do so.

If it should be the fortune of this book to lead to a further investigation of the question, to medical men and physiological inquirers this part of the subject will of course be left; the author can only regret that it is not already in better hands.

THE END.

INDEX.

A

B